"Hey, [...]
whispe[...]
you. H[...]
During the game, even! Man, he's confident."

"Kazuki... You sneaky..." All he could do in protest was move his lips. "Why would you do this while your're so angry?"

ONLY THE RING FINGER KNOWS

VOLUME 1
THE LONELY RING FINGER

Written by
SATORU KANNAGI

Illustrations by
HOTARU ODAGIRI

English translation by
Allison Markin Powell

DMP
DIGITAL MANGA
PUBLISHING
Los Angeles

ONLY THE RING FINGER KNOWS VOL. 1
THE LONELY RING FINGER

Written by Satoru Kannagi
Illustrated by Hotaru Odagiri
English translation by Allison Markin Powell

English Edition Published by
DIGITAL MANGA PUBLISHING
A division of DIGITAL MANGA, Inc.
1487 W 178th Street, Suite 300
Gardena, CA 90248

www.dmpbooks.com

Library of Congress Cataloging-in-Publication Data

Kannagi, Satoru.
 [Sono yubi dake ga shitteiru. English]
 The lonely ring finger / written by Satoru Kannagi ; illustrations by Hotaru Odagiri ; English translation by Allison Markin Powell.-- 1st ed.
   p. cm.
 ISBN 1-56970-904-1 (v. 1 : pbk.)
 1. Graphic novels. I. Odagiri, Hotaru. II. Powell, Allison Markin. III. Title.
PN6790.J34S6613 2006
741.5'952--dc22

                              2005031789

First Edition: April 2006
ISBN: 1-56970-904-1
10 9 8 7 6 5 4 3 2 1

Printed in China

Other ONLY THE RING FINGER KNOWS books
published by Digital Manga Publishing

<u>Manga</u>
Only The Ring Finger Knows

<u>Novels</u>
Only The Ring Finger Knows vol.1
The Lonely Ring Finger

Only The Ring Finger Knows vol.2
The Left Hand Dreams of Him

Contents

Only The Ring Finger Knows

"**I** mean, what I wanna know is, why are there people like that in the world?" Wataru's best friend Kawamura grumbled as he let out a sigh that reeked of alcohol. Since they had started drinking together in his room, Wataru had easily heard the same complaint at least a dozen times, yet he had the feeling that he would have to hear it again.

"Aww… If it were you, you'd feel the same, wouldn't you, Wataru?"

"Who, me?" Dodging the question, Wataru Fujii turned his dilated gaze toward his friend with annoyance, but still managed to dutifully grunt in agreement. "You're right, Kawamura, it's just like you say. That guy is tall, really smart, and as if that's not enough, he's hugely popular and handsome, too. He's just a perfect, incomparable human being!"

"Is that supposed to make me feel *better*?"

"Yeah, but…"

Showing his true colors, Kawamura pressed on as if offended. "Damn! I get it! Even you don't think I can compare with that guy, right?! That's it, isn't it? You can pick up chicks with your looks, Wataru, even if you happen to be clueless. You don't have to bother with that kind of thinking!"

"Pick up chicks? Where'd you get that idea, Kawamura…?"

"You're serious?! I get it. You don't think I hear what the girls in our class are saying? Seems like plenty of them whisper their concern over why you haven't taken off your ring after you and your girlfriend broke up."

"Oh, really?" This was the first he had heard of such gossip.

But because of his honest response, Kawamura became even more tight-lipped.

"Man…" He cursed everyone, and with tears forming in his eyes, he slugged down the can of beer in his hand. This ritual had been going on (and on) for quite a while—the floor around them was already littered with scattered piles of empty cans. "I mean, you with those big black eyes—they're a little intense, but they're still cute. And your face is small, too… I guess you're pretty balanced, but…"

"What do you mean, 'cute'? And anyway, what am I supposed to do about it, man?!"

"Oh, I get it," Kawamura gasped at Wataru's objection, as if he had suddenly sobered-up. Then the conversation went right back to the beginning, but now he started a bitter tirade.

"What I mean is, why does a perfect being like that guy have to exist, of all places, so close? Couldn't he be in show business? What is someone as gifted as Kazuki doing in a regular old private school like ours? And, what's worse, a year ahead of me?! Really, of all the unlucky…?!"

"Well, Yuichi Kazuki is kind of a celebrity at Ryokuyo High School."

"Every other month I hear that he gets scouted as a model. He could do it too, I bet."

Earlier that day, Kawamura had been dumped on account of that "gifted guy," so no matter how much he whined about his bad luck, it wouldn't change his mood. Wataru had been keeping him company on his drinking binge and complaint session since after school, but honestly, he was starting to feel annoyed each time the name "Yuichi Kazuki" came up.

It wasn't as if he couldn't appreciate why his friend was so bummed-out. Right after she dumped Kawamura, Mai Tachibana from their class admitted breathlessly that she was in love with Kazuki, which had pushed Kawamura to the bottom of this abyss of depression.

"How can she be in love with Kazuki…?"

Wataru's unsteady, glassy-eyed gaze fell upon the can of beer in his hand, and his head grew hot as he considered it. Even though Kawamura begrudged Kazuki, strangely enough hardly anyone in the whole school spoke poorly of him. It wasn't like he excelled at any particular sport or activity, but all of the teachers placed immeasurable trust in him as a student, and he was often brought out to play against other schools to make use of his all-around athleticism. Wataru didn't know him personally but the Yuichi Kazuki he saw from afar usually wore a familiar, gentle smile. He always carried an air of calm charm. Of course, he was naturally handsome, so much so that girls would giggle and melt just looking at him.

And even though he had a perfect reputation, Wataru thought, he didn't walk around with an entourage of hangers-on. His cool good looks stood out conspicuously in a crowd, but people around him seemed to insist on treating him normally. Wataru rather liked that about him.

But, of course, he couldn't say any of this in front of Kawamura.

"Ohhh… And I bought this pair of rings 'cause I thought the feeling was mutual. 24-karat gold?! All for nothing…" Kawamura muttered and sighed, his shoulders sinking. Rings were all the rage in their school, and the highest status of all was wearing matching rings. There were all kinds of special rules, like "single" or "currently seeking," that also applied. But whose ring sparkled on which finger was often the hot topic of conversation amongst all of the students, boys and girls alike.

"But Kawamura, don't you know the hard-and-fast rule?"

"What hard-and-fast rule?"

"Expensive gifts are taboo before you're officially an item. 'Cause then after you're together, she'll always bug you for fancy things. Got it?"

"Wataru…" Kawamura briefly wagged his index finger at him with a blank look on his face. Then, he opened his mouth, as if what Wataru said had made a deep impression. "Wataru... You're good. Somehow you don't fall for the girls' flirty advances, you stay aloof."

"Well, now you know why."

"Well... There's a rumor that you've still got the hots for your ex-girlfriend. Come on, take the ring off."

"But this ring's got nothing to do with Nano!" He had heard the same thing over and over by now, and it was starting to get to Wataru. Anyway, he was wearing the ring on his right middle finger, which meant he was single. "It's not like this is a pair with Nano's. That's not my style. In the first place, we talked it out and it was a mutual breakup. I'm free to wear whatever I want, wherever, aren't I?"

"But you've only got the one, right? Single guys usually have, like, two or three spares. You really take care of it, so that must be why they think that way."

"But it really *is* important to me." Wataru held his right hand in the air and gazed lovingly at his favorite silver ring. It fit his middle finger, and it was about 5 mm wide with a thin gold center line—a very simple design.

The time he had bought it did overlap with when he had been going out with Nano, which may explain why the false rumor was going around, but even still, Wataru had no desire to take his ring off. He wore it everywhere, even at school, and he took extra special care of it. It wasn't very expensive, but Wataru treated it like a treasured, sweet companion.

Kawamura clucked his tongue. "I had thought I'd be with Mai at least until summer vacation, which is why I bought these two rings..."

"I know, you already said so."

Now here was the one area he couldn't understand his psychology. For someone as independently minded as Wataru, he couldn't help but be disgusted by pairing up with someone like that. No matter how much Nano tried to coax him, he had refused to wear paired rings until the day they broke up.

But it would be cruel to say that to his broken-hearted companion. He pulled another beer from the liquor store bag and generously tossed it to his disheartened friend. "Come on, let's just drink tonight, okay?"

That was his duty for now. Resigning himself to it, he cracked open another beer with his fingernail.

This sucks. His head was pounding.

Wataru had been a complete wreck since he woke up. But after English made his eyes hurt even more, he finally caved-in and fell face-first on his desk during his free period.

"Hey, Wataru. Are you okay?"

Maddeningly, Kawamura seemed completely fine. Wataru glared at his friend with the happy-go-lucky voice and sprang to his feet with an angry sneer.

"Where ya goin'?"

"I'm...gonna go wash my face." If this didn't revive him, he'd have to skip his next class and go to the nurse's office. Making his mind up, he headed for the water fountain down the hallway.

The corridor was lit by calm, early summer sunshine, and Wataru let out a massive yawn. Since it was far away from the various free period activities, the only other person at the fountain was a tall male student.

"Man, I feel like crap..." He mumbled his complaint as he took off his ring and set it on the window sill. Since it was inexpensive silver and would tarnish easily, he had gotten in the habit of removing it whenever he got his hands wet. Standing next to the other student, Wataru forcefully turned on the tap and began thoroughly splashing his face with cold water.

"......!"

It seemed like the person beside him shrank back.

Oops, thought Wataru, quickly turning off the tap. He had been splashing pretty freely, and he had probably gotten the other person wet. "I-I'm sorry..."

As he hastily turned, his face still dripping, a gray handkerchief was held out silently in front of him.

"Want to dry off?"

"Huh?"

"Your bangs are soaked. It's all right, I didn't get splashed *that* badly."

"Th-Thanks."

The student handed it over with a gentle voice. It was neatly ironed and even smelled faintly of soap. Quite a contrast from Wataru, who kept the same wadded-up handkerchief shoved in his pocket day after day.

"Um... thanks a lot. I'll wash it and give it back to you if you tell me your name..." Feeling terrible that it was completely soaked, Wataru finally raised his head. But the instant he saw the person standing before him, his face completely froze.

"Yuichi... Kazuki..."

"Yes..."

As Wataru looked Yuichi directly in the eye, Yuichi's calm face instantly looked surprised. But then the smile disappeared from his lips and his eyes narrowed as if deeply troubled.

But Wataru barely noticed Kazuki's expression. The guy who Kawamura was bitching and moaning about all night was standing right in front of him! And he was even politely lending him his handkerchief! It was totally awkward.

"Ummm... Uhhh..." He was trying to stammer out a few words, when suddenly Kazuki's expression changed.

He gracefully crossed his arms and stared back at Wataru with a cruel look. Then he curled his lip and said, in a voice full of sarcasm, "Hmph! I've never been treated so casually by someone I haven't even met before. And by an underclassmen, no less!"

"Uh, no... I-I'm sorry!"

"Don't bother apologizing. When you see a celebrity on the street, I bet you're the type who points and shouts, 'It's what's-his-name!' Am I right?"

"Wh-Who does that kind of thing?!"

He involuntarily blushed at the insult. But in a voice that still seemed to be making fun of him, Yuichi smiled and said, "I wonder... Well, it doesn't make any difference to me. Because of your clumsy splashing, my uniform has gotten soaked... Whatever. Let me give you one piece of advice."

"Wh-What is it?"

"Wash your face at home."

As Yuichi peered down at him, Wataru got the feeling that he was just trying to show off how much taller he was. This was by far the first time he had experienced someone being so completely sarcastic toward him. Hadn't he always heard about the Yuichi Kazuki who was gentle and tolerant with everyone? Wasn't that why he had so many friends, both guys and girls, and why he was liked by both upper *and* underclassmen? But even if Wataru had addressed him casually by mistake, he didn't have to treat him this way, did he? And anyway, the third floor was for second-year students, so third-year Yuichi was actually the one who was out-of-place.

"It was too crowded on the upper floor, in case you were wondering. But don't worry, I won't come back." Yuichi lightly shrugged his shoulders and quickly turned to make his way upstairs.

Wataru called out to Yuichi's receding back. "Wait!" He turned around slowly, and his face was just as handsome as everyone said. "Y-You... You and that insulting tone, isn't that more rude than just acting casual?!"

"Huh?"

"And... You just keep saying 'You' and usually I'm..."

"Can you make yourself just a little clearer? Usually people don't mind when I say 'You.'"

"Wataru Fujii! My name is Wataru Fujii! Okay?! You'd better learn my full name!"

"Fine. Then this is for Wataru Fujii."

"Wh-What…?"

"*Don't* order me around." He spat out the words icily. Once again, Yuichi turned around and walked away. This time, no matter how much abuse the still-fuming Wataru heaped upon him, he was sure he wouldn't be able to stop him.

"Damn… What's with that guy…?!"

Left all alone, Wataru's distress somehow rooted him to the spot. When he recalled Yuichi's arrogant tone and his condescending attitude, he couldn't help but think that he wasn't anything like what people had said. "Or… Did I do something…?"

Knowing it was pointless to wonder, he was nonetheless speechless. Yuichi had been so kind when he offered his handkerchief, but the moment he saw Wataru's face, he became as nasty as if he had changed into another person. And even if he didn't like it when Wataru was familiar with him, wasn't Yuichi's transformation a huge overreaction?

His scornful glare, and his mouth quavering with that sarcastic smile… If that was Yuichi Kazuki, what had happened to the charming, smiling face he had seen before, he wondered.

The one thing that was true-to-form was his good looks. It was a shame, but the Yuichi seen up-close and personal was even more attractive than previously reported. That much Wataru couldn't deny. "They're fooled… Everyone's fooled by his looks!"

The kindness that was meant to charm everybody was in fact totally erratic. Wataru now knew from this experience how merciless he could be.

As the class bell slowly began to chime, Wataru realized that his anger had blown away his headache. He took his ring in his hand indignantly and hurried back to the classroom.

Since both of Wataru's parents worked, for lunch he usually grabbed something at the school cafeteria. But today

Kawamura's mother, who prided herself on her cooking, had been kind enough to make lunch for Wataru too, so he was grateful to be able to eat it in his classroom.

"What's up, you still have a headache?" Kawamura inquired after Wataru unintentionally let out yet another light sigh. When he opened his lunchbox, Wataru had exclaimed with such weird delight that it was no surprise his friend was concerned.

"I think I've gained weight."

"What? Gained where? If anything, you're skinny, aren't you? And you're short, too…"

"Didn't I tell you not to make fun of my height?! That's not what I meant… It doesn't fit…"

"What, your uniform?"

Wataru just shook his head wearily at that fact that his friend would just continue to reply this way. He dug his hand into the front pocket of his white shirt and pulled out the ring that he always wore.

"I don't get it… I went to put it on again after I washed my face, and now it won't fit."

"Wha—? Weren't you wearing it this morning?"

"I was. But I've always worn it on my middle finger and now it's a little tight. Even if I had to force it, I could always get it on. Isn't that strange, all-of-a-sudden? It fits on my ring finger, though…"

"Can someone gain that much weight so suddenly?" Not entirely convinced, Kawamura studied Wataru's ring. But a silver ring can't suddenly shrink, so it seemed like the only explanation was that Wataru's finger had, in fact, gotten bigger.

"And after your mother went to the trouble of making me lunch, I'm sorry… I've got to diet."

"Wataru… What, are you kidding? Where do you need to lose weight?"

"I told you, didn't I?! My ring…" Wataru was getting

irritated by the circular conversation, and had unconsciously started to lean over his desk, when suddenly the air in the classroom began to buzz with excitement as it filled from all sides with girls' voices in a rippling effect—"No way!" "But why?" "Seriously?!"

"Wh-What's going on?" Wataru drew back at the completely changed atmosphere as he followed everyone's gaze to the doorway. At the moment that he recognized Yuichi casually standing there, his heart began to pound involuntarily.

"What's that guy doing here?"

Was it his imagination, or did it seem like Yuichi was staring straight at him? *It couldn't be!* Wataru tried to deny it at first, but there he was—nonchalantly ignoring the forceful looks of the riveted girls. The sullen-faced Yuichi was unmistakably looking at Wataru.

"H-Hey... Isn't that Yuichi Kazuki?" Kawamura seemed intimidated as he whispered. It would be normal for him to think of Yuichi as his bitter rival in love, but instead he seemed to have lost his nerve in his actual presence. Wataru tried his best to pretend like he didn't know him, but on top of the fact that he couldn't ignore Yuichi's gaze, he was so physically uncomfortable he didn't know what to do.

"H-He's coming, Wataru! He's coming over here!" Kawamura was clearly upset. Nevertheless, Yuichi breezed right by Kawamura in his distress and stood beside Wataru, who continued to drink from his carton of green tea soymilk, feigning indifference.

"...Hey, you!"

"......"

"You can hear me, answer me."

"You know, I don't have to take this from you, didn't I tell you?" Wataru steeled his will and as he raised his eyes to meet Yuichi's. Against that very same will, he blushed. Although he would have expected such beautiful, clean-cut features to seem kind, there hung about Yuichi a surprisingly cold sharpness. Wataru understood in a flash that the reason could be found in those jet black eyes. What glimmered there was harsh, yet Wataru did not feel any displeasure. It seemed Yuichi's emotions were submerged in the slightest bit of color that remained on the surface, and Wataru wanted more than anything to be able to read what was reflected there.

Of course, Wataru had never been looked at in this way before.

"I-I said, uh… My name is…"

"Wataru Fujii, I know." Clearly annoyed, Yuichi rolled his eyes. Obviously he had not forgotten his name. He furrowed his brow sullenly and pulled something out of his own shirt pocket. "I came to return this."

"R-Return what?"

"We must've switched at the water fountain. You took my ring by mistake, didn't you?"

"Ring…? Huh?!"

"Put out your hand."

Shocked at being ordered around so arrogantly, Wataru automatically held out the palm of his right hand, into which was dropped a silver ring. It had a thin gold center line—it was Wataru's ring, all right. But the ring that he had just now been complaining about to Kawamura was exactly the same design.

Which meant that…

"Couldn't be… You mean, you and I have the same ring…?"

"…I'm not happy about it either," Yuichi said disinterestedly, crossing his arms with a frown. "That's enough, you're wasting my time. Hurry up and give me my ring back. You have it, don't you?"

"I have it… but… that's so…" Wataru, who had not yet recovered from the shock, stared incredulously at the ring in the palm of his hand. Until this moment he never would have dreamed that he had taken the wrong ring. Or rather, he couldn't believe the fact that he and Yuichi wore the same ring. "Uhhh… I thought I had gained weight or something… I always wear it on my middle finger, but for some reason today it only fit my ring finger!"

Yuichi made a somewhat twisted face at what Wataru said, but then, as if he had lost all patience, he thrust out his right hand with irritation.

"Whatever, hurry up and give it back. It's not as if I like wearing a paired ring with you, but a friend made that specially and it's precious to me."

"Y-You don't have to tell me, here it is!" Upset by Yuichi's persistent high-and-mighty attitude, Wataru tossed the ring he had back at him. *I'm the one who's not happy about having matching rings* he wanted to say while he had the chance. "That's it, isn't it? If that's all you came here for, hurry up and go. I can't deal with the way your mere presence makes the girls in the room go nuts!"

"You think I don't know?" Snatching up the ring roughly, he immediately slipped it on his right hand, as if to make sure that it was undamaged. The ring that had just barely gone on Wataru's ring finger fit as perfectly on Yuichi's middle finger as Cinderella's slipper.

Wait a minute… This isn't funny… As Wataru got more and more fed-up, he cursed Yuichi in his mind. How could the exact same ring produce such a different effect when it was worn by someone else? But that wasn't what really bothered Wataru.

He compared Yuichi's long fingers to his own stubby fingers with their short nails. With that silver accent, somehow even the movement of his hand was strangely captivating. He'd been nasty and rude and Wataru hated him, but the ring looked so good on him, it was as if it cancelled everything negative out.

"But…" A remark suddenly sprang to Wataru's lips. "Good thing you noticed that the rings were switched. It didn't even occur to me."

"Wouldn't anyone realize it the minute they tried it on? The only time I took off my ring was at the water fountain, and you were the only one next to me, weren't you? It's not very realistic to think that in half a day you got fat or something— what are you, stupid?"

"Stu-... What do you mean, stupid?"

"It was tight on you, right?" Yuichi glanced at Wataru's finger with that same condescending look. "On me, it was loose on my right middle finger. It fit perfectly on my left ring finger, though. My right and left hands have different finger widths."

"The left... ring finger...?"

"That's right. In other words, a place that's worthless for the ring to fit. That's why I had to get *this* ring back. It would cause a riot if I had to wear it on my ring finger. And anyway, it's creepy being paired up with some guy."

"Wh-Wha...? Well, same here!!" Wataru flashed back in a fit of anger, and Yuichi smiled faintly. Having got what he came for, he turned on his heel, but then, as if he had thought of something else, he spun around again.

"That ring... It's got a few years on it, huh?"

"Uh...yeah, I've always worn it. I like it, and I'm attached to it."

"Hmm...I thought so. It was so scratched up, I was impressed. I can see it's precious to you."

"Well...yeah, it is."

Since it was inexpensive silver and it scratched pretty easily, he couldn't really say that he took perfect care of it. But somehow that made him all the more attached to his own ring, so that when Yuichi told him he was impressed, he instantly felt oddly self-conscious.

While Wataru wondered how to respond, Yuichi tossed back a casual "See ya," and quickly walked away. The ring seemed to glint slightly on his finger, as if bidding farewell.

"What was that…?" Without thinking, the murmur escaped from Wataru's lips as he watched him leave. Yuichi had completely manipulated the conversation, and before he knew it, all that was left behind was the ring in his hand. Yuichi was the one who left the water fountain first, so of course, he was the one who had taken the wrong ring. Wataru had then simply taken the ring that was left, without any reason to doubt it was his. So what was that cocky, indignant attitude all about?

"He could have at least apologized…"

But that ring did *look good him, didn't it?* Clutching the ring in his grasp, he mumbled his confusing thoughts to himself.

"C'mon, you've got to tell me!" Having shown no sign yet of relenting her attitude, it looked like Mai might finally give up. As she loosened her overly familiar grip on his arm, she pouted the full lips of which she was so proud. "I told you, you're wearing the same ring as Kazuki. Well, that alone makes you the envy of all the girls! Don't you see?"

"Of course I see. But it's pure coincidence."

"Coincidence or not, the important thing is that it's the same ring. So I want the same one too. The least you could do is tell me where you bought it…"

"Sorry, but I don't remember. And anyway, it's bad enough that guy's wearing the same ring as mine. What, do you think I want *more* people to have it?"

Hearing Wataru's words, Mai suddenly stopped her flirty show and regarded him with a cold look. This morning, as soon as he entered the classroom, she had encircled him from behind, cooing "Fujii…" She'd thrown everyone else into a panic. *Really,* he wondered, *what did Kawamura see in this girl?*

Free at last, Wataru took a deep breath and headed over to Kawamura's seat. Because Mai had been flirting with Wataru, he was pretty glum. "Wataru, I'm begging you! Don't let Mai wear a paired ring with Kazuki!"

Hearing these as the first words out of his friend's mouth, he nodded deeply, but inside he had had enough. "Don't worry, I won't tell her. Anyway, I really don't remember where I bought it."

"Really? I thought it was important to you."

"It's true, but I've actually lost it once before. Then, suddenly, it just came back. After that, I got really attached to it."

"…I see. So what you're saying is, the ring is the same as Kazuki's, but the significance is different?"

"That's exactly what I mean." Gazing at the ring restored to his middle finger, Wataru gave a forceful, swift reply. After Kazuki came to see him yesterday, Mai and several other girls had approached him about the gossip, and he had brusquely rebuffed them all.

"It seems no one knew that Kazuki even wore a ring. That must be true… He's pretty popular, so I bet if he were wearing a ring people would talk about it right away. Maybe he used to just carry it around? Or, maybe he wears it but just takes it on and off to avoid attention. Don't you think he's kind-of a freak…? Well, he probably treasures his ring, too. So he didn't want it to get copied meaninglessly, right? Anyway, the story of you having paired rings spread almost instantly…"

"……"

Yuichi *had* come all the way to the second-year classroom to get it, so what Kawamura said was probably right. But that wasn't the only fact that Wataru found unamusing. Since Yuichi was the popular one, everyone thought that Wataru's ring was the copy. *Wasn't that completely ridiculous?* "Anyway, what a hassle!"

From a corner of the room, Mai was glowering at them both reproachfully. She *was* pretty, and her normally-mature attitude made her popular among the boy students, but even if she could get Yuichi Kazuki to be her boyfriend, it didn't seem like it would go so well. As one girl after another stopped Wataru to ask about the ring incident, he became more and more convinced of the height of Yuichi's popularity.

He's got everyone fooled, Wataru thought bitterly. He wanted to tell those girls whose cheeks flushed red as they raved deliriously about how wonderful Kazuki was just how nasty he could actually be. Everyone's favorite honor student—far from it! Wasn't the vivid glimmer in the look he gave Wataru proof of his secret, vicious nature?

"Now, now, just hang on 'til it all dies down. Cheer up!"

And just like that, their roles were reversed, with Wataru being consoled by Kawamura. But with such a difference between Yuichi's ring's influence and his own, he couldn't help but feel like his measly existence was rather insignificant. And even though Wataru was usually pretty cheerful, this was a somewhat disheartening reality.

There were two knocks on the door, and before Wataru could answer, the knob clicked and turned. With his headphones on, he waited silently for the intruder, and sure enough, his younger sister Karin quickly entered his room.

"Wataru, do you have a minute?" Karin smiled pleasantly at him and, as usual, sat down on Wataru's bed. She was a year younger and went to an all-girls school. "What are you listening to? Something new you bought?"

"It's the soundtrack to a movie I saw recently."

"Oh, the one you went to with Kawamura, right? Wataru, you still don't have a girlfriend, do you?"

"Mind your own business! I don't need a girlfriend, anyway. They're too stressful, and I can't be bothered!"

He took off the headphones and switched on the speakers. Instantly, the room was flooded with a lively Latin-style vocal. Karin tilted her head for a minute and seemed to enjoy the song. As her body moved slightly to the rhythm, she soon started talking again.

"You know, Wataru… Can I ask you to do me a favor?"

"I always know when you're gonna say that, just by that sickly-sweet tone in your voice. Depends on what it is. You can be pretty demanding, you know."

"Come on, don't say that, okay?" Her mascara-coated lashes curled up at him as she fixed her eyes on her brother. With her big, black eyes and strong, well-defined mouth, she really did look like Wataru.

"…I hate to ask but… Do you know a third-year at your school named Yuichi Kazuki? You must know him. Everyone does."

"Y-Yuichi Kazuki?!"

"That's right. So, you see, I guess it's this Kazuki guy's birthday soon, and a classmate of mine asked me to forward a gift to him but…"

"Now, wait a minute, Karin…"

"I'm sorry, I know. You hate this kind of thing. I told her you wouldn't. But this girl, it's like she's obsessed with him, so… It just slipped out that you go to Ryokuyo High."

If he only listened to what she was saying, it sounded credible, but when he looked at Karin's face it was obvious that she didn't feel bad at all. And once she had started in about a "favor," he knew very well that it would be impossible to refuse.

There was nothing he could do—Wataru sighed while he looked back at Karin's face. He knew he was no match for her in this discussion. "So, what then? For that guy's birthday?"

"Born in June, he's a Gemini, blood type A—I hear he's the second son of a dentist. Well, he gets high points just for that! On top of that, he's tall and gets good grades, right? Wataru, if you have a friend like that, why don't you ever bring him home? Don't be rude!"

"That guy's not my friend!"

"Really? But by the way you muttered 'that guy' I figured you were pretty close."

"W-Well… But…" Wataru gave a bitter smile and avoided Karin's innocent remark. Because he was wearing paired rings with Yuichi and had attracted the attention of the girls at his school, it wasn't surprising that he felt miserable and didn't want to talk about it any more.

"Anyway, I'm asking you to do this for me. There's a letter inside, so I think Kazuki will contact her after you give it to him."

"Why? He might just ignore it. That guy gets so many gifts, I'm sure he could sell them for profit."

"But I've heard he's not that cruel." Karin just grinned as she made what to Wataru was a completely maddening comment. According to what she had heard, for every letter or present Yuichi got from the many girls, he gave each one a proper, polite declining answer.

"But why not just refuse them? What a drag…"

"I don't know why. Most guys would just ignore the whole thing. Maybe it's part of his act, but if someone gives you a gift you should at least say thank you. And turning someone down is pretty hurtful, isn't it? They cry and all. There aren't many guys who'd apologize and say 'sorry' when they haven't done anything wrong."

"I guess you're right…"

"You can understand, can't you, Wataru? You decline a lot of things." Karin knew all the details about Wataru's love life since kindergarten. It wasn't as if he had anything close to the number of admirers that Yuichi had, but she was keenly aware of the number of girls that he had rebuffed.

"So anyway, it's a deal! Tomorrow, the girl will give me the present." Having strong-armed a promise out of him, Karin stuck out her pinky and exclaimed with a smile, "Yeah!"

Forced to link fingers with his little sister, Wataru swore a pinky-promise with a dark mumble and a heavy heart.

"But I love you, Kazuki," Mai said, as she started to cry.

With an upward glance through her wet lashes, she looked at Yuichi, calculating that she was most beautiful from that angle.

"Sorry, but I can't return your feelings, no matter how many times you profess them. Sorry, Tachibana-san."

"You mean... There's no chance at all?"

He shook his head no, and she tried to throw herself into his arms. But just before she did, he gently caught her with both arms, and unfortunately her attempt ended in failure.

"I really am sorry. I'm sure you understand." Smiling whether she did or not, Yuichi had deftly avoided her ulterior motive. She gave up her pretense and cast her eyes down, seeming at a total loss.

There, in a corner of the same room...

This is no good... No good... Without thinking, Wataru almost spoke out-loud as he hurriedly clapped his right hand over his mouth. He was clutching to his chest the wrapped present that Karin had gotten yesterday. The package was an armful, so he guessed that it probably contained clothing.

If possible, he didn't want to hand it over in front of other people, but he hated sneaking around after Yuichi. Wataru had innocently followed him, wondering what he could be doing in the calligraphy studio after school, but before he could call his name, Mai came in. Wataru quickly hid behind a desk, but now it would be even more difficult for him to emerge. He was at a loss.

Can't tell Kawamura about this... Nevertheless, as he listened to what transpired he was rather impressed. Yuichi wasn't popular with the girls for nothing, and his rejection was flawless. With his kind voice and soft gaze, he firmly asserted a strength that left no room for argument.

"Hey."

"......"

"Hey, Wataru Fujii. What're you doing over there? Don't tell me peeping is a hobby of yours?"

"Huh? Argh…!" Bumping into the desk, Wataru jumped up, startled. Without having noticed it, Yuichi was now looking down on him.

"Fancy meeting you here."

"Ah, um… Well, actually…"

"By the way, carrying that big package makes you look even smaller."

His uncalled-for jibe incensed Wataru, but then he remembered Mai. As if reading his mind, Yuichi said, "She's gone. …But really, what are you doing here? You weren't following me, were you?"

"N-No way!! That's not it… Tachibana… That's right, I was worried about Tachibana…"

"Worried?"

Forced into a corner, Wataru made something up, and Yuichi narrowed one of his eyes suspiciously. But all Wataru could do in this situation was keep lying. "I-It's true. My friend has a crush on her so he asked me to check up on her…"

"So, that means you knew that she would come talk to me today. That gives me the creeps…"

"I-It's not like I wanted to witness that. To begin with, you may act all cool, but inside aren't you regretting it?"

As Wataru spoke, Yuichi really seemed to get annoyed. For the first time, Wataru saw emotions clearly displayed on his face. *What is it…? Up to now, he had such a gentle look…* Wataru was sure that Yuichi hadn't had this sulky look in front of Mai. If it had been him standing there, he couldn't have helped but been annoyed by a girl's tears, but Yuichi had let her cry it out while kindly watching her.

So then, what was the big difference?

Wataru felt overwhelmed by an uncontrollable anger. All of a sudden, he was smacked roughly on the head. He looked up and saw Yuichi gazing at him with his brows furrowed.

"What's the big deal?!"

"Sure, I'm not some cute girl. And I'm sure it cramps your

style to wear the same ring as me!"

"Huh? What's gotten into you?"

"Nothing! I give up. I'm leaving!"

Damn, he hits pretty hard... Cursing him in his mind, Wataru turned to go but suddenly he was grabbed by the wrist. Wataru tried to break free but he was held by a surprising strength, and he ended up facing Yuichi. "What are you doing?!"

With a fierce look, Yuichi scowled at him, but he seemed to hesitate for a moment. Surprised, Wataru looked back at his face again, but his expression had already returned to its former surliness.

"Listen." Yuichi's pupils glittered sternly. "Don't ever follow me again. If you don't leave right now, I'll tell everyone you're a stalker."

"I wasn't... It was Tachibana..."

"You suck at lying."

The soft voice, the gentle tone—none of that was ever intended for Wataru. Yuichi used harsh words to demonstrate make the point. With a light thump to his chest, he silently urged Wataru to go. And as Wataru shrank back, powerless, he began to feel sad for no reason at all.

What did I ever do to you...? He really wanted to ask, but no matter how he tried, his mouth was frozen and he couldn't speak. Hugging the present he forgot to give to his chest, slowly he turned his back on Yuichi.

I know those who see me probably get the wrong idea. Probably 100% of them get the wrong idea. Wataru's mind was racing as he proceeded to the third-year classroom, unable to muster his courage. *I don't care if anyone misunderstands,* he thought, but when that person might be Yuichi, he got upset all over again.

But, it does bother me that everyone will think I brought that guy a birthday present... Whenever anyone passed by Wataru his heart wouldn't stop pounding, but he couldn't wander the halls forever, and lunch hour was over. There was still a little time left before Yuichi's birthday, and Wataru wanted to fulfill his obligation as soon as possible.

If I can just get this over with, I'll be free... That was his only consolation now. Wataru had been deeply hurt when Yuichi had called him a stalker, so he made a decision to give up the games and play by the rules. *I'll just hand this off and leave right after, and then I'll never have to see that Kazuki again.* He no longer wanted to be at the mercy of this new ache in his chest that he didn't understand.

"Kazuki? Yeah, just a sec." His friend answered pleasantly as he went back inside, just after Wataru finally summoned his courage and asked for him. Well, at least he had cleared the first hurdle.

He felt somewhat relieved, and soon Yuichi appeared with his usual evident reluctance.

"You again?" He sighed as if to say, *Give me a break,* as he coldly looked down the ten centimeters between him and Wataru. It might have been the difference in the light, but Yuichi's face looked rather more tired than usual.

Wataru suddenly got worried—he lost his nerve and stood there speechless. But when Yuichi laid his eyes upon the package in Wataru's hands, in as hateful a tone as ever, he said, "Well, well, Wataru Fujii, the mighty gift bearer. The ribbon is a pretty girly touch, but somehow it strangely suits you."

"Wh-What?!"

"...I don't know... You've been roaming around with that thing for quite a while now, haven't you? You sure you aren't funny that way?"

"Wha—... I'm just..." Having taken the bait of his provocation, Wataru quickly regained himself. If he wasted time with this kind of thing, then everyone would *really* start gossiping.

"What's the angry face for? Is there someone in third-year you want to give it to? You want me to deliver it for you?"

"Wh-What changed your tune?"

"Huh? Haven't you heard? I'm a *nice guy*. Don't you know my rep?"

"I completely forgot about that the moment I met you." *I really wish I could forget,* Wataru thought sadly to himself. *The guy standing in front of me with the coldest eyes is kind to everyone but me… It's really a fact I'd prefer not to acknowledge.*

Better hurry up and get out of here, Wataru thought, making up his mind as he thrust the package towards Yuichi's chest. "Here. It's your birthday soon, right?"

"What…?"

"I've delivered it properly. So accept it gracefully."

"…For me?"

It seemed like this was completely beyond Yuichi's expectation. He was rendered speechless, and he hesitantly reached out his hand towards the package. When his fingertips touched the present, his eyes began to glisten the slightest bit, and his expression—which up to a moment ago had been so somber—suddenly seemed to take on a beautiful glow.

Such a genuine expression, Wataru thought with surprise as he watched him. *He's so popular he must be really used to getting gifts, but could it be that he acts this surprised every time?*

"Uh… That's, you see…" If he didn't speak up, he might end up just standing there, dumbstruck in admiration, so he hastily stammered a command. "Umm, respond to that promptly, will you? There's a letter inside…"

"A letter? Is that your style?"

"D-Don't ask me. Just read it and you'll understand it all. I'm just…"

"Fine. So I should just read it?"

"Yeah… That's right…"

While they were talking, Wataru started to get the most baffling feeling that it was he who was giving Yuichi the present. Or at least, that was the impression he got from the look on Yuichi's face. It was almost as if he didn't know if he should show his happiness at this unexpected gift. This was the first time he had seen this fresh, new expression. Without that gentle smile or a trace of that ironic look, he saw Yuichi's true feelings.

Disarmed, Wataru realized his grave error. He had yet to mention anything to Yuichi about who the gift-giver was. "Uh... W-Wait!" He said without thinking. "Th-That present... It's not from me! D-Don't get the wrong idea!"

"What idea...?"

"I mean, I was just asked to give that to you by some girl who goes to my kid sister's school... She basically forced me to..."

"Oh, I get it." Yuichi readily accepted Wataru's explanation, seeming almost disappointed. Darting his eyes at the package, he asked, "What's inside?" His voice was already back to normal.

"I have no idea. I didn't ask."

"That's irresponsible of you. What if this was a bomb, and it was the work of someone who had a grudge against me. Wouldn't you feel responsible?"

"A grudge? No one has a grudge against you, do they? Aren't you the one with the honor student rep?"

"I wouldn't say that." With a bold look and a faint smile, Yuichi folded his arms around the present. "I'm popular. I could have made enemies without knowing it."

"......"

Normally something like that could only be taken as a joke, but the fact that Yuichi had dared to say it made it strangely convincing. The lovely color had completely left his face and the sinister glint was back in his eyes. Taking a step to close the distance between them, Yuichi backed Wataru up against the wall.

"Do you know when my birthday is?"

"J-June the 7th..."

"Bingo. Good for you." Yuichi thumped his right hand against the wall and just stared at Wataru. He was so close that he could feel his breath. If he had wanted to escape he could have, but for some reason, Wataru couldn't tear himself away.

"Thanks for the special delivery." Moving his lips slowly, he spoke without his eyes smiling at all. "But you sure are a pushover. Wasting your lunch hour running errands for some girl you don't even know. You really must be bored."

"Don't speak to me that way! And I told you, I just promised my sister that..."

"Did you ever think it could be your little sister?"

"What?"

"The present could be from her, and she's just saying that it's 'from a friend,' when in reality she's the one with the hots for me. Well?"

Wataru was as surprised as when he had been insulted. He felt the blood rush to his head. With the cold wall at his back, Wataru stared at Yuichi, who looked like he was having more and more fun. The corners of his mouth slowly turned up.

"I didn't know you had a sister complex, kid."

"Don't call me a kid!" Saying he had a sister complex was extremely unsettling for Wataru—since he and Karin looked so much like each other it was as bad as being called a narcissist.

Yuichi squeezed Wataru's shoulder hard and whispered, "Then what should I call you? You seem to hate whatever I call you."

"W-Well... How 'bout 'Junior Fujii'?"

"'Junior Fujii'?"

"No, well, never mind the junior part. If not that then... Hmm..."

"How about 'Wataru'?"

All of a sudden they were on a first-name basis. As soon as he said that, Yuichi brought his head close to Wataru's ear. Feeling Yuichi's soft breath, Wataru reflexively stiffened. In a low, raspy voice, he moistened Wataru's ear with the most dangerous word of all.

"Wataru…"

"Uhhh…" Hearing his name spoken so meaningfully, all at once Wataru's body temperature rose. This was a pleasure he had never experienced before. Wataru was overcome as the warm sensation gradually spread throughout his body. His will now taken captive, he couldn't even look at Yuichi. All he could do was hope that this wave of pleasure would soon pass.

"Wataru?" He had looked away without budging an inch. Yuichi let go of the hand that held his left shoulder and reached towards Wataru's chin. But as Wataru noticed the ring on his finger, he roughly pushed it aside.

"C-Cut it out!"

"What?! All I did was say your name."

Wataru's frustration mounted at Yuichi's brusque response. Even if he were to demand, *Just now, what were you going to do…?* he knew that Yuichi would quickly read his mind.

"You suddenly froze up. I wanted to see your expression. What, did you think I was gonna kiss you or something?"

"I-I didn't say that…"

"Really? Then why are you blushing. What happened to your attitude, Wataru?"

"Don't call me that!"

"You complain too much. Besides, you're the one who's being overly familiar with an upperclassman. Think about it!" Grinning, Yuichi suddenly thrust the present back at Wataru's chest. Just as he was leaving, he said hastily, "Here…" as he turned with a dismissive gesture. "Sorry, but I don't feel like carrying it. I can't accept it. Return to sender."

"I can't do that! I thought you accepted presents from

everyone?!"

"Well, it's true, I don't play favorites."

"Then, why…?!"

"There's a very simple reason." Yuichi paused and stated impassively, "Because you were the one who brought it."

"But…"

"Tell them if they want to give me something to do it themselves instead of asking someone else. Oh, and about the name thing…"

"What…?"

"You can call me Mr. Kazuki."

"……"

While Wataru stood there dumbstruck, Yuichi calmly headed back to the classroom. With a straight spine, he cut a fine figure from behind. Somehow even his plain uniform seemed stylish; the white summer shirt looked better on him than anyone else.

But inside, he's the worst, Wataru muttered, stunned. According to Karin, he was the kind of person who would properly accept and politely thank someone for a gift, or so they said. Since Yuichi had refused this gesture, had he done something wrong? All Wataru could think was that Yuichi must really hate him. *Yeah, he must…* Didn't he say flat-out that he wouldn't accept it because Wataru brought it?

"Karin's gonna kill me…"

But that wasn't the only reason for the ache in his chest. At the time, though, Wataru didn't know enough to realize it.

"I can't believe it! Wataru, what did you do?! I'll totally lose face!!" Just as he thought, Karin got home and he was immediately showered with a volley of verbal abuse. "You've always been like this, Wataru. People think you're likable and you've got plenty of friends, but there's this cold side of you, you know?"

"What does that have to do with this?"

"Everything! Even with Nano, you suddenly broke up with her, saying you weren't sure if you really loved her or not. I bet you've never even seriously felt love for anyone before. Isn't that why you're so indifferent?"

"Karin, I told you, that guy Kazuki, he's not the great guy you all think he is, you know?"

"Who's interested in a guy who won't allow himself to be idealized?!" Looking aside, she fell silent for a moment. *Finally*, Wataru thought, relieved. But then she said in an inscrutable voice, "Hmm... Isn't it unlike you to just come slinking back, after having the gift thrown back in your face? Are you *that* kind of person?"

"Forcing a gift on someone who doesn't want it is insulting, isn't it?"

"I guess so, but..." With a dissatisfied look on her face, Karin tied on an apron and began to prepare dinner. Since their mother often worked late, Karin usually took over the evening meal at their house. But it looked like dinner tonight would consist of all the things that Wataru disliked. "You know, Wataru..."

"What?"

"Well, I hate to say it, but do you think Kazuki *really* hates you? That's what it seems like after hearing your stories."

"......"

"On the other hand..." Taking the onions that Wataru hated out of a grocery bag, Karin smiled meaningfully. "...maybe he *really* likes you, Wataru?"

With a heavy heart, Wataru dragged himself to school and forced himself to open the door to the classroom. His classmates, who had been chatting amongst themselves, glanced up at him and then made a point of averting their gaze.

I thought so... His shoulders drooped dejectedly at the unsurprising development. When he got to his seat,

Kawamura, who was already there, hurried over with an excited look on his face.

"Wataru, you…"

"Stop! Everyone doesn't have to know! It's true, I took a gift to Yuichi Kazuki, and I'm the first person in history to have that gift thrown back in my face!"

"Huh? Did that really happen?"

"What?" It seemed a different rumor that Wataru didn't know about was making the rounds. He looked back at Kawamura and asked in a low voice, "Wait, what are you talking about?"

"Well, it does involve Kazuki… Yesterday, after you went home, he came to our class! You didn't know?!"

"Kazuki?! Why?"

"He asked me to tell him which school your sister goes to, with this really serious look on his face. It was almost as if he waited for a time when he knew you wouldn't be here."

"What is that guy thinking…?" Maybe because of the way Wataru mumbled sullenly, Kawamura seemed to feel somewhat responsible.

"Sorry, I just went and told him," he said apologetically. "Ever since the ring incident, I thought you guys were through, but I guess you two still connect, huh?"

"*We do not!*"

"But you gave him a present, right? Come to think of it, this morning, I did hear a rumor that Kazuki even had male admirers now… Sooo, that was about you?"

"Don't be so easily convinced!!" Wataru hastily explained the story behind the present, anxious for Kawamura to understand. But it wasn't as if he could go around the whole school making excuses, so he wouldn't be able to stop the rumors entirely.

"Don't worry." Kawamura casually sat down on Wataru's desk, consoling him with an easygoing look. "By now, the story that Kazuki came asking about your sister should have gotten around. Everyone will conclude that Kazuki is after Karin, and the whole matching-ring incident will be chalked up to being about your sister!"

"You think so…?"

"It's much more believable that Kazuki would be in love with your sister than with you. No one will think anything of a brother handing over a present from his little sister, right? And since Karin goes to another school, she won't be troubled by any gossip here… It's all good!"

Listening to Kawamura's story, Wataru realized why Kawamura seemed to be in such a good mood. If Kazuki had a love interest, Mai would have to give up on him, wouldn't she? And even if it was just a rumor, Kawamura could still put the moves back on her. "Kawamura, you really are…"

"What?"

"…faithful to your desires, aren't you?" Wataru smirked, impressed.

"Yeah!" Kawamura said enthusiastically, giving him a thumbs-up.

"C'mon, seriously?" Wataru sighed wearily while standing and facing the books on the top shelf. It was depressing enough that he had to be in the dust-filled library craning his neck so much it hurt, and he hadn't even eaten lunch yet. "Tachibana must be skipping class duty."

Maybe his partner Mai was angry about the news about Wataru and Karin, and had abandoned her work and disappeared somewhere. Now Wataru would have to carry all the materials for the first afternoon class by himself. He had the list from the English teacher in his hand, but Wataru was already discouraged.

"What am I supposed to do about all these books? I mean, really…" But because he was too humiliated to say anything, he simply stood there staring at the bookshelf, biting his lip. He couldn't reach them. Probably because they were seldom-used English books, all the books on the list were on the highest shelf of the row at the very end. When he tried to get one of them down, his fingertips could just barely reach the spine, which put Wataru in an even fouler mood.

"Why is this happening to me…?" Wataru clucked his tongue and looked around for a stepladder. Since he never really came to the library he didn't know where anything was, but as far as he could tell, there was no stepladder to be found. It looked like he was going to have to climb up the bookcase. He really didn't want to, but there was no choice. Wataru looked up again to confirm where the book was, and put one foot on the shelf.

Just then he heard, "Which one?"

Wataru was so surprised to hear the brusque words all-of-a-sudden that his heart nearly leaped out of his chest. The impulse almost knocked him off-balance, and he came dangerously close to falling over backwards. But he was narrowly caught and avoided being flung onto the floor. Breathing a sigh of relief, Wataru cautiously raised his gaze… and then panicked. "Wh-What are you doing here?!"

"I should ask you the same. I thought you were the least bookish student in the school, so what do you think you're doing?"

When he saw that the person who saved him was Yuichi, Wataru was highly confused. He hurriedly pulled himself up and out of Yuichi's arms and frowned as he said, "Th-Thanks… a lot…"

"You're welcome," Yuichi answered nonchalantly, quickly turning his gaze back to the shelf that Wataru was staring at so intently. "So, which one is it?"

"Huh?"

"The book. You wanted it, didn't you? Tell me, and I'll get it for you. *You're* not going to be able to reach it, are you?"

"Mind your own business!"

"And the stepladder's broken," Yuichi said, driving his

point home as Wataru choked on his words. Treating him like a pipsqueak made him angry, but the real problem was that for someone as short as he was, getting the books down from the shelf would be an extremely difficult task.

"It's better than climbing, isn't it?" Yuichi smiled brightly as if he were playing with Wataru, and grabbed the list from his hand. "This brings back memories. I read these same books last year, too. This list is from Suzuki, the grammar teacher, right?"

"You read…? But it's in English."

"Using a dictionary, yeah. Read 'em once through, write a report and you might even have a shot at a top university." Skillfully taking down each book, Yuichi handed the last volume to Wataru, who for some reason couldn't just blithely respond to his joke.

"Um… Can I ask you something?"

"Sure."

"Why are you being so nice today?" He dared to force out his question as Yuichi shut the book whose pages he had been flipping through. A slight wrinkle furrowed his brow, and after a considerable silence, he spoke while carefully choosing his words.

"It would be a problem if these reference books weren't prepared, wouldn't it? From the looks of it, you were the only one here."

"Yeah, but…"

"I had no choice: I spot a small fry who's having trouble reaching the books. I happen to be there. And I also happen to know that the stepladder is broken. So of course, I have to help. Don't worry, I didn't do it just because it was you."

"But you could have ignored me…"

"What are you saying? You're irresponsible. If the reference books aren't ready, the whole class suffers, right?" There was no room to argue—it was the perfect answer. Yet Yuichi's bold words were completely belied by his uncomfortable expression.

He probably feels really awkward... He'd been so nasty all along to Wataru, and although it was by chance, the fact that he had to be nice to him now probably bothered Yuichi a lot. *It's because you're so strangely serious about certain things,* Wataru thought, which struck him as so funny that he almost burst out laughing, despite himself. It was true. What Yuichi said made sense, but if he really was a jerk, he would have just ignored him no matter what the reason was and continued on his way. *Maybe this guy's just really stubborn...* Stealing a glance at his profile, there wasn't a hint of concern for Wataru. Yuichi seemed like he was trying desperately to keep up a stern facade.

Wataru had seen this exact expression before. As he realized this, he remembered the moment when he had given him the present. Yesterday, Yuichi had had precisely the same look on his face. It was as if, through a crack in his expression, Wataru might catch a glimpse of his real emotions, and he was troubled that he couldn't hide them. Wataru wondered what triggered it. *Is it...me?* As he mumbled the words, his heart raced.

He could have been totally wrong, but his heart began to throb the moment the thought occurred to him. *It can't be that he showed such emotion because he thought the present was from me...* If that was the case, then maybe Yuichi didn't hate Wataru after all. His heart beat even faster at the slight, newfound hope. But even if he wanted to confirm such a thing, Yuichi wouldn't give him an answer, would he? He'd probably just glare more coldly at him. That's what pained Wataru even more.

He gave up any further thought of it and decided to bring the stack to the classroom. But just as he'd feared, there was no way he'd be able to carry such a mountain of hardcover books all by himself. He was at a loss, until Yuichi, who had lapsed into silence, uttered, "Want me to help you?"

"Huh? Would you really?"

"Only if…" From under the now-familiar sullen face, a brilliant smile crossed his lips. "…you bow your head and ask nicely."

It was the next day after school. As they came out of the classroom, Wataru and Kawamura were talking about stopping for some fast food on their way home. Suddenly, they became aware of an odd commotion that stopped them in their tracks. Looking around, they saw hordes of girls rushing down the stairs with anxious looks on their faces.

"Is there something going on?" Kawamura called out to one of the girls, who looked back distractedly.

"Don't you know? The basketball team is playing Kaisei High in a practice game in the gym."

"All this just for a practice game…?"

"Of course! Kazuki's in the game! His friend on the team asked him to play as a stand-in. It's started already…" She trailed off as she hurriedly left them. Kawamura elbowed Wataru as he asked, "What do you wanna do? Should we swing by the gym?"

"Seriously? I thought you didn't like Kazuki."

"Well, yeah… He is my rival in love…" Kawamura seemed to hesitate until the hallway had emptied before adding, "Well Wataru, you look like you want to go."

Wataru's school was a university-feeder institution, so it was kind to say that they had a decent basketball team. Nevertheless, the score was 20-38, and Ryokuyo had an overwhelming lead.

"Hey…! We're not so bad after all," Kawamura said, impressed, as Wataru sat next to him, brooding, with a confused look on his face. *How did I end up here in the gym,* he wondered. *Doesn't this only confirm Kawamura when he said, 'You look like you want to go'? What was I thinking?*

Even though he was just a reliever, Yuichi was the team's

star player. As he ran up and down the court, he looked so effortlessly cool. It was fascinating for anyone to watch him play, and Wataru felt a thrill in his chest. *This* must be the Yuichi Kazuki that everyone knew and loved so much.

I wish it were enough just to look at him... While Wataru got lost in his thoughts, a cheer went up from the crowd. Yuichi had scored again. The pair of girls right in front of him clapped their hands while jumping and screaming.

"Hey Wataru, did you see that?" Kawamura whispered through the noise. "Kazuki spotted you. He glanced over and gave a little smile. During the game, even! Man, he's confident."

"Seriously…?" Somehow, to have Yuichi think he had come to cheer him on bothered Wataru a little. With that arrogant look on his face, he'll probably just start teasing again.

But if he put aside his feelings and watched the game, Wataru had to admit that Yuichi's playing was spectacular. He was so much better than the other players that he couldn't really work any combination plays, even though there were many opportunities. Yet, Yuichi wasn't irritated—rather, he seemed to be enjoying the game. Maybe that was why the other players also seemed relaxed and excited to be playing.

"Doesn't he seem…too perfect?" He heard Kawamura mutter this to himself, despite being surrounded by cheers as if they were at a teen idol concert. The game was already in the second-half and their lead had only widened.

But why did that "too perfect" being take such a hostile attitude towards Wataru? He had yet to unravel the mystery. Yesterday in the library, Wataru felt like he had caught a glimpse of his true nature, but now, at this distance, he was uncertain again. The kind, thoughtful, and serious student… or mean, haughty, and ill-tempered…he never, ever shows his true colors… *Which is the real Yuichi?* he wondered.

"Awesome! Another basket!" At some point Kawamura had been drawn into the game, and now he raised his right fist in a victory pose. Yuichi had scored dozens of points on his own, and now everyone was convinced that Ryokuyo was going to win.

…But.

Suddenly Yuichi stood still and raised one hand to stop the game. As his teammates and the spectators waited to see what would happen, Yuichi hurried off the court with a stoic expression.

"What? Did he get injured or something?"

"Injured?" If that was case, he wore a pretty calm expression. As Wataru noted Yuichi's face as he walked off, he thought, *Maybe*…

Ryokuyo's substitution player was called from the bench. Starting with Kawamura, a loud cry went up from the students who had gathered in the gym, but there were less than five minutes left in the game. As it stood, Ryokuyo could probably still win even without Yuichi.

But the one who had done the most for the team was no longer on the court. Wataru scanned the bench and saw him finish a short conversation with the coach and then leave without waiting to see the rest of the game.

"Kazuki…" At that moment, Wataru wanted to run after him, not caring what people would think. Even though it was Yuichi who had roused the game to this point, Wataru had a feeling he understood why he had left just before they were about to win.

"To suddenly be replaced like that, something must have happened. Don't you think, Wataru?"

"Sorry, Kawamura, I've got to go!" As he ran out distractedly, he wondered if he had been too abrupt. The crowd who had come specifically to see Yuichi wondered whether to stay until the end, but surprisingly few people decided to leave.

Changing into his sneakers as he burst outside, Wataru held himself back while he looked all around. Yuichi had left just moments ago, but he was nowhere to be seen. "No way... Why isn't he here?" The schoolyard was quiet, as if the furor inside the gym had been a dream, which made Wataru feel all the more helpless. "What... Where did he go...?"

"Looking for me?"

Hearing a voice behind him, Wataru was so surprised he was unable to turn around. Before his frozen body went back to normal, he realized that someone was slowly approaching him from behind. "Kazuki?"

"That's Mr. Kazuki to you." His laughing voice melted into the summer evening. Enveloped by the grape-colored sky, Wataru suddenly wanted to crouch down in that spot like a child. If he turned around, he knew Yuichi would speak harshly to him like always. But the voice he heard now was ever-so gentle.

"I was right."

"Huh?"

"I knew you would run out after me," Yuichi said as he tapped Wataru, who still hadn't looked at him, on the shoulder. "You came rushing out, didn't you? What a fool... This will be the first win for the Ryokuyo team since forever. How could you miss such a historic moment?"

"Kazuki..."

"You're ruining your shoes." As Yuichi pointed out, in rushing out after him, Wataru hadn't bothered to put his shoes on properly. The Etonics sneakers he had saved up his allowance to buy were now all smooshed up at the heels. Wataru bent down awkwardly, and for some reason Yuichi squatted down beside him. His basketball uniform fluttered in the breeze, and even though it was almost summer, there was something cold about his sweaty skin. For some reason the line of his round, bare shoulders made Wataru uncomfortable as he retied his shoelaces in silence.

"The game should be over soon."

"You don't fool me, Kazuki. You were planning to leave

before the end all along, weren't you?"

"What?"

"The game. Why did you bother at all? They're winning because of you. I bet the team wants you to play through 'til the end."

"I got bored," Yuichi said breezily, his expression either serious or joking. *Once again shrouded in the mist*...thought Wataru as he gave him a harsh look. Yuichi shrugged his shoulders, "It would have been annoying if I'd stayed."

"That's not…"

"No, not for them. I meant me, I'd be annoyed."

Just then, a loud cheer shook the gym, and they could hear the whistle ending the game. Judging from the liveliness, it appeared that Ryokuyo had won. Soon enough, the other students would start filtering out with excited looks on their faces.

Yuichi let out a sigh and slowly stood up. As Wataru did the same, Yuichi's eyes fell upon Wataru's sneakers. "Those are cool," he said, giving him an unusual compliment. "Slight frame, clunky high-tops… The contrast fits your personality to a 'T.'"

"What's that supposed to mean?"

"That you're rough and unrefined."

Wataru thought about how their different-sized rings looked so elegant on Yuichi that it was like they weren't the same ring, and he really couldn't argue with him. Instead of opening his mouth, he scowled at Yuichi with a disgruntled look.

"And that is a most predictable response." Despite being scowled at, Yuichi seemed happy somehow. He ran his long fingers through his bangs and, looking up at the darkening sky, murmured softly, "I'd better get changed."

Hey... As Wataru noticed that Yuichi wasn't wearing his ring, he was suddenly overcome with a feeling of loneliness. While the same ring was still snug on his middle finger, what had Yuichi done with his? He almost felt as if he had lost his other half. *Oh yeah, like Kawamura said, he must just carry it around...* But still, the sight of Yuichi's bare finger was somehow sad. For Wataru, who had always hated having the same thing as someone else, this was a major change of heart. He could not understand why he was so upset by a single ring.

"What? The ring? I took it off for the game," Yuichi said suddenly, as he waved the fingers of his right hand in front of Wataru's eyes. "Too bad for you I didn't lose it, huh?"

"No, I…"

"I could tell right away from the way you were staring— man, you're easy to read. Fortunately, I'm not so stupid that I'd lose it again."

"…So I'm stupid."

"Huh?"

"I've lost it once before."

Yuichi's fingers stopped moving at Wataru's answer. He silently urged him on and Wataru continued, bewildered. If he wasn't careful, Yuichi would make fun of him again. He felt uneasy inside, but surprisingly Yuichi earnestly tilted his head to listen to his story.

"This was about one or two months after I bought it. Same thing. I lost the ring at school. You see, I took it off to wash my hands like last time, and left it there. It wasn't that expensive so, I gave up on it pretty easily… But then a week later, it just came back."

"Came back?"

"Yeah. I still don't know how but I came to school one morning, and there it was on my desk. I was so surprised. It was almost like the ring came back to me on its own and well…I was moved…"

"I see…"

"Since then, I've treasured it. 'Cause wouldn't you be happy if you got back something you'd already given up on? When I look at this ring, I can remember that feeling…" At some point Wataru became aware of how passionately he was speaking, and he blushed and shut up. *Was that childish…?* He cringed with self-loathing.

But Yuichi, who had been silently listening to him speak, softly repeated, "Something I'd given up on…"

"Yeah, I guess that would make me happy."

"What…"

"But if you ask me, it's too bad for you that we have the same design. That ring looks way better on me, doesn't it?"

"Kazuki, how dare you…"

"That's 'Mr.' to you, Wataru. In spite of your looks, your personality's not cute at all."

"Cute…?! Don't say cute!! It gives me the chills! Anyway, you…"

"I said you're *not* cute, didn't I? Stop ranting and listen."

The more worked up Wataru got, the more provocative Yuichi's taunts became. It had finally been going well, but in the end, Yuichi acted like it was all a big joke. Wataru had run out because he had been worried about him, and now Yuichi just thought he was a fool.

"Just to let you know, I'm never taking this ring off again! So of course, that means I'll never lose it either! I have more of an attachment to this ring than you'll ever have, so I pray with each passing day you'll get tired of yours! And the fact that we have the same design really gets on my nerves!" Wataru gave himself over to the momentum of the words that he didn't really mean and carried on, even though they contradicted his feelings from just a few moments ago. But he was afraid that if he didn't act this way, Yuichi might find out that he felt like his ring was his own's other half.

As a brief silence fell between them, for the first time Wataru noticed how dark the sky had gotten. The area in front of them got noisier and students began to file out of the gym. The two of them were in a spot that wasn't visible from the front door and it was pretty dark around them but, not knowing whether anyone could see them, Wataru grew more and more uncomfortable.

"Well, I'm leaving now." He wondered what kind of rant he'd spew the next time he saw Yuichi, as he hurried to disappear into the crowd.

And then.

"K-Kazuki…?"

His wrist caught firmly, Wataru couldn't move. He rushed to free himself from this unexpected development but the force that held his wrist was surprisingly strong and he couldn't break free easily.

"Kazuki… What…?!" Wataru was frightened by Yuichi's eyes. His fierce gaze was fastened on his middle finger. There was the same silver ring that Yuichi had taken off. "Wh-What… Are you mad?" To his horror, he could hear his voice trembling slightly.

Yuichi pulled on Wataru's wrist, tugging his whole hand out of the shadows. Then, very slowly, Yuichi slid his gaze from Wataru's ring to his eyes, where they held for just a moment.

"You just won't shut up," he murmured in a low voice, as he swiftly moved his lips to Wataru's ring. It happened in such a flash that by the time Wataru came back to himself, his wrist had already been released.

"Serves you right," Yuichi said, moistening his lips with his tongue and smiling boldly.

But Wataru still couldn't believe what had just awakened in his body. His right hand was trembling just a bit, as if to prove that Yuichi's kiss was real.

The smile gone from his lips, Yuichi watched Wataru's stupefied state for a moment. Then, as if giving up on something, he sighed ever-so-slightly. Quietly he faced the procession of students and started walking, and as the sharp-eyed girls surrounded him, he disappeared from view.

That jerk… He's just making fun of me… When he thought about it, Yuichi was always like this. He said what he wanted

to say, did what he wanted to do, and then left Wataru all riled-up while he disappeared! He was sure that the next time he saw Yuichi he'd act another way and confuse him. What does he mean, 'serves you right'? He wondered what Yuichi thought of the ring that had touched his lips. Since it looked just like his, he figured it could only be an object to provoke offense.

And since I'm the one wearing it... He really didn't want to think as much, but it was all he could come up with. Wataru had said how much it bothered him to have the same ring, and Yuichi probably felt the same way.

"Maybe," Karin had said innocently, "he reeaally hates you, Wataru?"

She must be right, Wataru thought, clenching his still-trembling right hand. He stood there, rooted to the spot.

The next few days were torture for Wataru. Just as Kawamura had predicted, the fact that "Kazuki came to ask about Karin's school" was completely distorted into "Kazuki is dating Fujii's little sister," and had spread throughout the whole school. He might have been able to handle it if he just had to deal with Mai but, facing the entire female student body, it was painful for him to pretend like he didn't know. Countless times he had been pulled aside, called out to, and even given looks full of hostility. Almost all of the questions were to determine whether the rumor was true, but it had been Kawamura's idea for Wataru to maintain a noncommittal attitude, neither confirming nor denying it. The strange thing was, by doing so, people usually tended to think the worst, and he was fed up with girls bursting into tears.

"But, any rumors about your ring have disappeared. Isn't that what you wanted?"

"Well, now none of them will talk to me at all."

That was about the only good thing that he could say about it, which probably suited Kawamura just fine, he thought bluntly. It was likely Kawamura attributed Wataru's recent lack of energy to his involvement with the rumor. As the sunshine beat down relentlessly in his classroom during free period, the strong light reminded Wataru of early summer. It seemed that simply looking at its intense glare would be enough to rob him of his spirit entirely.

"I didn't really believe it before but, that Kazuki really is popular. He's gained even more fans since the basketball game."

"Even though he left mid-game."

"Wataru, you went chasing after him, didn't you? You surprised me, man. So, what was the reason for his exit?"

"How should I know?!" Wataru said grumpily, pouting.

To Wataru's surprise, Kawamura nodded his head in agreement. *What?* Wataru asked with his eyes, as Kawamura smiled, as if he knew what was going on. "He probably said something to you, baiting you again, right? C'mon, Wataru, you're not still mad from before. Honestly, listening to your stories, you guys are like schoolchildren."

"That jerk Kazuki's just taunting me."

"I don't think so. I think he's just having fun because you take the bait so easily. I don't think anybody else knows about this childish side of Kazuki. I mean, I haven't seen it for myself, so it's hard to believe."

"......"

"Wataru?" Kawamura leaned forward in his seat, bringing his face close to Wataru's. "Umm, it's just a hunch, but could it be that you don't like the rumors about Kazuki and Karin? 'Cause it bothers you to use her as a pawn..."

"What gave you that idea?"

"'Cause you look so grumpy all the time."

"I always look this way!" Wataru stood up with a jerk and roughly grabbed his bag. He still had class, but he had no desire to stay at school.

"H-Hey! What's the deal?!" Wataru ignored Kawamura's

surprised voice as he left the classroom and hurried off as fast as he could. He wanted to get out and put at least a little distance between himself and everyone who couldn't stop talking about his connection with Yuichi.

Of course, there wasn't a shred of truth that Karin and Yuichi were dating. If she found out, she'd probably fly into a rage, and Kazuki would just grin. The whole thing was just a random remark manipulated to Kawamura's and Wataru's advantage. Nevertheless, each time he answered, "Those two... I don't really know," somehow it became more unbearable for Wataru. It was as if he himself was starting to believe it was true.

I feel so stupid... Wataru got tired of running and, hanging his head, he silently trudged along the asphalt. If he felt stupid, on the other hand, what exactly did he want to do? He repeated the thought over and over, cross-examining himself.

Just like Kawamura said, he was right that it would serve them to be vague about the rumor for a while. Wataru didn't want people thinking about the ring or the present incidents, and Kawamura could have a consolation match with Mai.

But Wataru still did not feel better. Even though they wore the same rings, people just saw Karin's shadow behind him. They were assured that he was just a "friend of the kid sister's boyfriend." For the many who were in love with Yuichi, even though they saw Karin as a threat, Wataru wasn't a problem since he was a guy.

Of course not, Kazuki and I are both guys... Despite this fact, his wounded self still felt awful. Just imagining the difficulty of fulfilling their relationship made his head hurt. Someone as popular as Yuichi had no reason to choose another guy for a partner.

There's gotta be something wrong with me... Thinking of Kazuki and himself in a romantic situation was clearly proof that his head was a mess. No matter what, it would never happen. Wataru couldn't even guess what Yuichi thought of him—whether he liked him or hated him.

Of course, he couldn't fathom his own feelings either. When Yuichi had whispered his name, he had felt that rush. Even now, he could vividly recall the pleasure. But that didn't mean that he was in love with him.

The path that ran along the tracks towards the station was lined by well-known cherry trees. As he passed underneath the glimmering greenery, Wataru felt slightly comforted. *I bet it would be picture-perfect to walk here in spring with Yuichi through a rain of beautiful cherry blossoms.* But as his imagination got carried away, he realized that by spring of next year, Yuichi would be graduating, and his heart grew heavy again.

There really is something wrong with me... It's been less than two weeks since we met and started talking... And yet, he felt like they'd been playing jokes on each other since they were kids, and Yuichi felt dear to him. This was not at all strange to Wataru. *That's right, then...*

Wataru came to a halt. Tomorrow, Sunday, was finally Yuichi's birthday. He wondered what Karin's friend, whose present had been refused, had done about it. *Well, that's got nothing to do with me!* Shaking his head from side to side, he started walking again. It was none of his business if some girl's advances on Yuichi failed. Right now, what was important to Wataru was his old, peaceful student life. If he was to get back to it, he would have to tolerate the rumor, even if it was about Karin.

But whether or not his "peaceful student life" was what he *really* wanted, Wataru could not say for sure.

"I'm home." It was past five in the evening by the time Wataru walked in the door. Whether or not he had skipped class, if he had come straight home he wouldn't have had anything to do, so he had stopped to see a movie. The arthouse cinema was showing an Italian film that had lightened his mood and Wataru, now slightly revived, was greeted by Karin in high spirits.

"Welcome home, Wataru! I'm making dinner now." Stirring a pot, Karin looked back genially at Wataru as he peered into the kitchen. Staring at her, he could see how much they resembled each other. Karin's hair was thicker than Wataru's, which was soft and fine, but her short, bouncy hairstyle suited her bubbly personality.

"So, tonight it's Wataru's favorite, minestrone and chilled pasta with clams! Oh, there're onions in it, but I'll take out the ones in your portion, okay?" She really seemed like she was in a good mood.

As Wataru sat down in a dining room chair, she turned off the heat and cheerfully approached. "Thank you, Wataru. You followed up on that business with Kazuki for me, right?"

"Followed up? About what?" Just hearing the name Kazuki from Karin's lips made Wataru's heart ache so much he thought it would break. At that moment, Wataru was keenly aware that the person who was most uncomfortable with the rumor about Yuichi and Karin was *him*.

"Didn't Kazuki ask you something? Today, he came down to my school. He said, 'You're Miss Karin Fujii, aren't you?'"

"Kazuki… At your school…?"

"Uh-huh. I think he waited by the school gate until I came out. He must've cut fourth period, otherwise there couldn't have been such good timing."

"I cut, too…"

"What?"

"Nothing. So, what did Kazuki want with you?" That's what he really wanted to know. Amid all the confusion, he had totally forgotten that Yuichi had come to ask about Karin's school in the first place, and now he was about to find out.

Karin must have been proud that someone as talked-about as Yuichi had waited for her. Her cheeks were faintly flushed, and even the tone of her voice was higher than usual. It pained him to see that Karin had no idea she was already known as Yuichi's love interest at her older brother's school.

"Kazuki came to apologize to my friend, but he didn't know her name so he thought he'd ask me, he said."

"Then it was about the gift? He told me to take it back because he didn't want to carry it. You wouldn't believe how arrogant he was about it."

"Yeah, he said he wasn't feeling well that day. But he said he was sorry he took it out on the present and he apologized."

"The present?! He apologized about the present but not to me?! Damn! What's up with him?! He has no idea what I went through to…"

"H-Hey, calm down, Wataru." Karin seemed taken aback by Wataru's sudden rage. Compared to her own usual clear-cut temper, Wataru was the one who always kept his own feelings in-check. She had seldom (if ever) seen this kind of anger in her brother. "Anyway, he said that he also wanted to apologize to the girl with the present, and then he called her from his cell phone."

"So then what happened?"

"With what?"

"You know what I mean, the outcome! Is Kazuki gonna go out with that girl? Or…?"

"Wataru…" Karin fell silent for a moment as she watched the anger in Wataru's dour face. "Hey, isn't that kind of strange?"

"Strange? Karin, what do you mean?"

"When you said it like that, Wataru… It's like you're jealous…"

"……"

"That's jealousy. You're jealous, aren't you?"

"W-Wh-What…?" That was definitely not a word he wanted to hear. But his own sister had tossed it out, and now waited for a response with an expression as if nothing had happened. Wataru had instantly turned white, and no matter what lie or excuse he made up, his face gave her the answer.

"Yes!" she shouted. "Ohhh…I *knew* it!"

"Huh?"

"So I put you in a painful position, huh? Sorry, sorry!"

"K-Karin…?" *What did she mean, she **knew** it?* He wanted to snap back, but to his regret he didn't have the nerve. Wataru smiled bitterly as his sister apologized, since this wasn't so different from how he had felt earlier today.

"Actually, I was a bit suspicious. I thought maybe your own feelings had kept you from delivering that present…"

"Karin! I told you—I would never do something so cowardly! And what do you mean, 'feelings'? What feelings?!"

"Okay, okay, I get it. Settle down. You're so easy to read! It all must be clear to Kazuki by now. Or have you already confessed?"

"O-Of-Of course not! What would I confess to him…he's a guy! Karin, how can you say that to your own brother? C'mon, think rationally!"

"You're the one who's got to be rational, Wataru! The whole reason Kazuki came to see me was because he had made you look bad. As usual, he politely declined on the spot to my friend. There, do you feel better now?"

"He… declined…?" As soon as he heard Karin's words, it was like a tense string snapped. Wataru looked at her face like he had lost his wits and couldn't speak a word.

Am I… Am I… Jealous…?

"Are you in love with me?" He was sure Yuichi would ask nonchalantly, intently watching Wataru at a loss for an answer. He would probably use all of his charm to easily extract the words "I love you" from Wataru's lips. His power was that great.

"Wataru, are you okay?" Karin's voice sounded like noise to Wataru. He was struggling with all his might against the head-spinning impact. The vision of Yuichi in his head, while spitefully watching Wataru, smiled gracefully and said, ***"Are you in love with me...?"***

Wataru put on the ring he had taken off before bed and checked his reflection in the mirror one more time.

"...All right." He thought his hair, tousled with wax, made him seem twice as handsome as usual. Taking a soft, deep breath, he grabbed his blue, nylon shoulder bag and went outside.

The onset of high summer was still far-off, but maybe because the rainy season was late starting there had been fine weather every day. Today was Sunday. Even Wataru's gait couldn't help but be lighter.

"Let's see...Fifth Street. That's pretty close." Wataru had found Yuichi's address in the school register and although it was a little set-apart, it was still in his neighborhood. Wataru had decided to pay him a visit on foot while taking a walk. He still wasn't really sure what he would say to Yuichi, but Wataru wanted to see him. Once they were face-to-face, there were things he wanted to discuss.

"Apparently, he's spending his birthday with his family. I guess it's their annual tradition. Their relatives come over and it's a big to-do. High society, huh?" When Karin told him that, Wataru had instantly thought about going to visit Yuichi. Yesterday he had totally gone along with what Karin said, but honestly, Wataru didn't even understand his own feelings yet. He never imagined that he would fall in love with another guy, and there was still a part of him that didn't want to accept it. If he could just see Yuichi's face, Wataru hoped that it would clear away this fog.

But once I'm certain, then what will I do...? Another part of him rationally wondered about his next move. Either way, for now, Wataru could only keep walking. Even before earning Yuichi's love, or finding out if his feelings were mutual, first he wanted to know his own true feelings.

When he had been with Nano, Wataru's heart had been filled with calm. Perhaps because she was his first girlfriend, he had thought it was love, but eventually he began to feel out-of-place with the calm. When he was dealing with Yuichi, it didn't go that way at all. Now he felt like these feelings of love for another person were completely different from his usual, serene temperament. It was like an emotional rollercoaster that left no doubt about the excitement.

It's right there if I cut through the park. Wataru had come upon a soccer field that had been set up as a playground and he decided to use it as a shortcut. Maybe he was nervous; he was suddenly very thirsty.

Looking around for a vending machine, he spotted a kids' water fountain in the distance and headed in that direction first. *The first time I met Kazuki was at a water fountain…when he lent me his handkerchief.* His angry exchange with Yuichi seemed like such a long time ago. Thinking back, a wry smile crossed Wataru's face.

Humming as he neared the fountain, Wataru reached his hand toward the tap. Just then, a familiar voice reached his ears and he froze where he was.

"No, no, Toko. It's much quicker if we cut through here. No matter how many times you come over, you always forget."

"Sorr-y! And as for you, you're still rude, Yuichi. Will you ever stop? You just like to contradict me."

"Okay, okay, I know."

The bright, cheery voices were approaching Wataru from behind. Not wanting to be seen for some reason, Wataru made an effort to seem casual as he turned to face the jungle gym.

That's Kazuki's voice, but… He was supposed to be at home celebrating with his family. As if answering Wataru's question, he heard Yuichi's voice again. "Everyone will be glad. It's been awhile since you've come to the house."

"My pleasure. After all, it's my favorite guy's special day."

Watching them from afar, the girl Yuichi was calling Toko seemed easily three or four years older. Judging from their conversation, she must have come over to celebrate his birthday and Yuichi had come to meet her. There was no way for Wataru to tell from looking, though from the way they were chatting pleasantly they seemed like close siblings. But Karin had told him that Yuichi didn't have any sisters, and the two of them didn't resemble each other in the least. Toko was pretty, to be sure, but compared to Yuichi's conspicuous good looks, the guy definitely won out.

Wataru watched them, hoping that they'd leave soon, but ironically Yuichi came and stood by the same water fountain. Toko joined him and they stood there talking.

"And how is it? Is the ring okay?"

"Yeah, great. See, I'm even wearing it now. There was a little incident and I even started wearing it at school. Thank to that, my hand's completely used to it now. Looks good, huh?"

"Well, it looks like you're taking good care of it."

"Of course."

Wataru couldn't believe what Yuichi said next to the pleased-looking Toko. "After all, it was a present from 'my dear Miss Toko.' I treasure it."

"Well, I put all my love into it, you know." They looked at each other and burst into hearty laughter at the same time. Even Wataru could glean enough from this conversation to tell that the ring symbolized a deep bond between them.

But...

At some point Wataru had tightly clenched his right hand into a fist. There, on his middle finger, shone the same ring as Yuichi's. The other day, Yuichi had ended up kissing Wataru's ring after he had blurted that it got on his nerves to have the same one as him. But really, it made Wataru happy to have matching rings..that's what he had planned to admit to Yuichi today when he saw him.

Yuichi glanced at his watch and hastily urged Toko to start walking while Wataru watched the two of them, unable to move a single finger. Yuichi put his arm around Toko's shoulder, and her body language made it seem like this was the most natural thing in the world. There was no reason to think they were related.

Kazuki... Wataru wanted to shout out to him and draw Yuichi back, if he could. That was the desire at the bottom of his heart as he parted his trembling lips. But he couldn't risk making a fool of himself, so he just watched their retreating silhouettes as they got smaller and smaller.

Left alone, Wataru felt the presence of someone else and lowered his gaze. There before him was a cute little five-year-old girl in a pink dress. Her hair was tied in two ponytails with ribbon that matched her outfit, and with her little arms and legs she was trying to climb up the iron bars. Maybe because of her ruffled dress, she seemed rather precocious. Wataru instinctively put out his hand and helped her up to where she wanted to go.

"Thank you." She hadn't gone very high, but still she seemed happy. Looking down on Wataru, she continued. "Mister, what are you doing?"

"Me? I'm...going home."

"Home? Is it close by?"

"Yeah, real close. What about you?"

"Mom and Dad and Puru and Takako, we came by car—to Grampa's." Since it seemed like she was done with the jungle gym, Wataru took the hint and helped her back down. The girl smiled pleasantly. "Puru is my dog. It's called a miniature long-haired dachshund, do you know it?"

"Wow, you remembered such a long name. Good girl."

"Takako is smart."

"I know... As a reward, I'll give you this." Wataru plucked the ring from his middle finger and quietly dropped it into the palm of her hand, held open like a maple leaf.

She stared at the ring, puzzled for a moment, and then she pouted her lips and whined, "This is too big!"

"That's okay. You can wear it when you grow up. So keep it safe 'til then, okay?"

"Are you going to marry Takako? Is this a wedding ring?"

"Marry you? Yeah, okay... Let's do that." From her innocent words, suddenly Wataru was about to cry, but he barely managed to hold back his tears.

The girl slipped on the ring that was too big for her and cheerily ran out of the park. Only after she was far away did she turn back to wave "Bye-bye!" and then her tiny shadow was gone.

"Bye-bye..." The ring no longer shone on the hand that he raised to wave goodbye. Since she had said they came by car, he would probably never see her again. All too soon, Wataru had been parted from his precious ring. He closed his now-unadorned fingers and softly put his lips to the spot that Yuichi had once kissed. There was only the bitter taste of silver where the ring had left a red mark.

"Is Wataru Fujii here?" Yuichi shouted as soon as he opened the classroom door and barged in. In such a strange atmosphere, even the girls in the class, who would normally flutter about, fell silent as if they had lost their nerve. Yuichi's sharp eyes quickly spotted Wataru standing and talking by the window and, ignoring the gazes upon him, Yuichi grabbed both of Wataru's arms. Taken aback by this unexpected development, it took Wataru quite awhile to realize that it was Yuichi.

"Hey! If you're here, at least answer!"

"Wh-What's going on?! Let go!"

"Sorry, but I can't do that," Yuichi retorted, dragging Wataru by the arm as he started walking away. The one o'clock class was about to begin, and Wataru wondered where he could be taking him. Judging from his tone, Wataru imagined the worst. He had never seen Yuichi behave so roughly, and his own protests were pretty weak.

"What do you think you're doing?! Hey, Kazuki…!"

"I want a word with you. Shut-up and follow me."

"This is so unfair…!"

"I'm pissed off," Yuichi stopped for a moment and looked at Wataru coldly. "So I'll say this ahead-of-time. I might do something awful to you."

"What?!"

"It's just the heat of the moment." Maybe it was odd how completely pale Wataru's face went, but Yuichi narrowed his eyes slightly. And with that, Wataru was dragged off by Yuichi in front of all his classmates.

"C'mon, seriously, where are we going?"

"……"

No matter how many times he asked, Yuichi wouldn't say where they were going, so in the end Wataru gave up and allowed himself to be pulled along. On their way the first bell rang, but of course Yuichi didn't seem to care as they rushed down the stairs from the third to the first floor. The only rooms on that floor were the nurse's office, the art room, special classrooms, and the exhibition room—places where hardly any students went during the day. Yuichi appeared to be heading for one of these rooms as he made his way along the corridor without hesitation.

What's going on…? This morning, Wataru would never have dreamed he'd be forced to cut class and dragged to a deserted room. Actually, in the three days since the weekend when he had seen Yuichi with Toko, Wataru had hardly seen Yuichi's face. Looking at him even now it was painful, and Yuichi was still wearing proudly wearing the ring on his finger.

"Go in." Yuichi had opened the door to the student council office and urged Wataru ahead of him.

Wataru's arms, now released, still hurt where there were grip marks. "Are you on the student council…?"

"No. Why would I bother with that kind of extra work? The president's a friend of mine. He lets me have a spare key."

"I remember the story now. You got the most votes but they were all considered invalid."

"Of course. How could I win if I wasn't even running? …Sit down."

Wataru had never been inside the student council office, but Yuichi seemed at home as he brought over one of the tubular chairs. This must be where he came when he decided not to go to class. Inside the desolate room was a large square conference table with tubular chairs, and on the walls there were only steel bookshelves. For some reason, Wataru couldn't relax.

"So… What did you want to say?" Wataru timidly shifted his weight as he sat down in the chair offered to him.

Yuichi rested his hand on the back and leaned over to whisper, "Don't play dumb. You know what this is about, don't you?"

"Huh?"

"So tell me… When exactly did I start dating your sister?"

"Oh… Th-That's…" Wataru, with his broken heart, had completely forgotten about the rumor that was still going strong at school. It must have finally made its way to Yuichi himself.

"Because of that, I just had the worst birthday ever. Thanks a lot—I owe you."

"The worst…? Um, did something happen?"

"It doesn't concern you. But someone did tell me that they asked her brother, Fujii in second-year, if it was true and he didn't deny it."

"……"

"*You* spread that rumor, didn't you?" Yuichi sighed heavily and then he put Wataru's downcast chin between his fingers and turned it up towards him. "Why such a dark face? I'm the one who should be depressed. It's bad enough how much fuss everyone makes, but now that you've added fuel to the fire, I can't take it anymore."

"I'm sorry." Unable to shake off his fingers, Wataru tried desperately to look away from Yuichi. But instead Yuichi, not yet satisfied, came even closer and peered into Wataru's eyes.

"Why didn't you tell the truth when they asked you? Do you really want your sister and me to be together so badly?"

"But... You went to see her, didn't you?"

"What?"

"Karin told me all about it. You went to her school, Kazuki. You even cut fourth period to go... What were you thinking?"

"What do you mean?"

"What happened on your birthday? Does it have something to do with the rumor? If it does, then I..."

"Wataru, your brain must be really puny. How many times do I have to tell you? It had nothing to do with you," Yuichi said in a cold voice as he grabbed Wataru's small head with his long fingers. Wataru may have gotten used to such rough treatment, but this made him angry.

"That's enough! Let go! Let go, I said! Jerk! Pervert! Freak!"

"Well, you seem lively enough."

"Knock it off! I don't have time to argue with you! I've had nothing but bad luck since I switched rings with you! Go to hell!"

"Would you *really* say that?"

Wataru knew he sounded like a little kid, but it seemed to have had an effect. In fact, it seemed like his abuse was somehow refreshing to Yuichi, who didn't usually hear such invective from other people.

Finally freed from Yuichi's grasp, Wataru asked the same question again while trying his best to fix his disheveled hair, "What happened on your birthday?"

Since he had seen him looking so happy in the park with

that older girl, he wasn't going to let him get away with saying he had had a bad time. Hinting at his meaning, Wataru slowly stood up from the chair. "You dragged me here just to complain about your birthday?! What are you, a little kid? Stop griping about it!"

"You're the one who's acting like a little kid, Wataru."

"Uh…"

"Never mind that, answer my question. Why did you spread that rumor?"

"I told you… That was…" Facing each other straight-on, the difference in their height was at least ten centimeters. Looking down on him, close enough to feel his breath and still unable to tear his gaze away, no matter how hard Wataru stood his ground it was still painful. "…Because people got the wrong idea."

"Huh?"

"Stories about us having the same ring, and my bringing you a present. I was tired of people talking about stupid things like that! But if a story that you had a girlfriend got around, then no one would bother with rumors about me, a guy. Anyway… none of that matters now."

"Doesn't matter… What do you mean?"

"I got rid of the ring. Threw it away. So now I don't have to worry about any more gossip, and I don't need to rely on any rumor to help me out either."

"You threw it away?" Yuichi gasped, dumbfounded, and opened his eyes wide like he couldn't believe what he had just heard. All expression disappeared from his classic features. "You threw it… What are you saying…?"

"It's true. So from now on, Kazuki, you don't have to be annoyed any more. Are you happy now? It's the precious ring you got from your girlfriend, right? I'm sure it really bothered you that it was the same design as mine."

"Wataru…"

"It's fine. I mean, mine was something I bought at random.

But Kazuki, yours is different. It would be a real shame if you lost yours, since it's a special ring. Aren't you glad? Now that my ring's gone, that one is yours alone." While he was speaking, the image of how happy Yuichi and that girl had looked flooded his memory, and even Wataru felt less and less sure of what he was trying to say.

What Wataru did know was that he was in love with Yuichi. Watching them walk away that day in the park, he had finally realized that. He knew it was pathetic that it had taken a broken heart for him to admit it, but this was the first time Wataru had really fallen in love.

"Let me see your hand," Yuichi uttered after a long silence. "Wataru, your right hand, let me see it!"

"No."

"Show me!" As he roughly grabbed his hand, Wataru instinctively looked away. He was afraid to see what Yuichi's face would look like when he saw his bare finger.

"I don't believe it…" The stunned words fell from Yuichi's lips. Still holding Wataru's hand, his eyes were fastened so directly on Wataru's completely empty middle finger that it almost hurt.

As Wataru slowly raised his face, his heart felt crushed to see how Yuichi mourned the loss of his ring as if someone had died. "Kazuki, I…"

"You idiot… Why would you go and throw it away? When did I ever say that it annoyed me to share rings with you?"

"No, I… It was me… I didn't like it."

"But you didn't have to get rid of it!"

"No, that's not it!" Shaking his head vigorously, Wataru interrupted Yuichi. Why was it true that the more real the feelings were, the harder it was to express them? The Yuichi he loved was standing right in front of him but no amount of words would grant him Yuichi's heart. Wataru's feelings were bound up with the ring, and now he would probably never again have either of them.

"Your ring and mine, they're not the same. They're completely different, I understand that now. But when I found out, it pained me to wear my own ring so…"

"Found out? Found what out?"

"Your true feelings. You…"

"Huh?"

"That you're not looking…at me." By the time the words came out he realized it was too late.

Wataru tried to shut up, as his bound right hand waved about. Without a word, Yuichi pulled him closer and forced him into an embrace.

"I'm…?" Yuichi's voice trembled sadly, which made a beautiful resonance in Wataru's ear. "You think I'm not looking at you…?"

"Kazuki…"

"Wataru…you're an idiot." Holding his head and turning it upwards, Wataru reflexively closed his eyes. His eyelids were dampened by Yuichi's breath, and little by little Yuichi slowly lowered his lips onto Wataru's. Their hot breath intermingled, as their body heat shot up. Wataru felt completely swept away. It was that passionate a kiss.

His breath was enveloped by Yuichi's soft touch, and while his head spun, Wataru tried hard to concentrate on what was awakening in his body. But then another kiss followed, and his reason and resistance completely melted away. Yuichi's lips felt warm on his, and Wataru gradually opened his heart to this pleasure. When Yuichi drew his lips strongly into his own mouth, Wataru felt a sweet numbness all the way to his fingertips, and he sighed deeply over and over, enraptured in Yuichi's arms.

In the silence, his heart was beating furiously and Wataru tried to bring his consciousness back to reality. As he felt the touch of the ring on Yuichi's hand that was holding his back, he awoke from his dream with a start.

"Wh-What are you doing?!" He shoved Yuichi's body

away and bit his own lip to try to shake off the sweetness that lingered there. Wataru did not miss the sadness, the faint trace of bewilderment that floated in Yuichi's eyes as he stared at him silently. "You bastard! If this is a bad joke, well, I'm not laughing!"

"Then what? You wanted a laughable kiss?"

"I don't want to hear it! You hurt me, you jerk! Pervert! Letch!"

That ring that you always keep so close, you love it because you got it from her. The words nearly got stuck in his throat. Wataru stared back at Yuichi, who was looking at him with a disappointed expression.

But maybe, just maybe, if I reached out to him now... The thought quickly flashed in Wataru's mind. Maybe, even if it's a million-to-one chance, Yuichi might take his hand. In the moment that thin hope was born in his heart, it was extinguished before it could even take shape. Sighing lightly, Wataru tried his best to control the tumult inside him as he said, "I apologize about the rumor. I'm sorry."

"It doesn't matter now."

"It *does* matter! I'll tell everyone myself that it was untrue. And about Karin…"

"What? You want to arrange a marriage between us or something?"

"No, nothing like that. Uh, you went all the way to her school to straighten it out for me, right? She was happy about that so…thank you," Wataru said, bowing his head.

Yuichi turned aside, seeming disturbed. He pushed back his bangs with his long fingers and murmured wearily, "You and your sister, you really look alike."

"Yeah… We often get mistaken for twins."

"I knew it was her right away just by looking at her face. I've got it. If I start going out with your little sister, that rumor will become the truth, right? Why don't we do that?" Yuichi suggested in a reckless tone, turning back towards Wataru.

"It's a good idea, isn't it?" The twisted smile on his face contradicted his words. "Then everything will work out. Right, Wataru?"

"What are you saying?"

"I'm serious. She's pretty cute. And I like 'em stubborn. On top of that, the fact that she looks like you would be fun."

"F-Fun…?"

"To continue this romantic scenario with your little sister."

Slap!

The lively sound tore through the air and rang in the closed room. Yuichi's left cheek reddened instantly before Wataru's eyes.

"Kazuki, we're through!"

"……"

"I never want to see you again! My ring is gone too, so that's just fine!"

"Hey, what are you… Just hold on!"

"No! Goodbye, Kazuki!"

Having been slapped and renounced, Yuichi looked quite panicked—not like himself at all. Probably no one but Wataru had ever seen such an uncool Yuichi Kazuki. In the end, it was worth it just to see his expression.

Leaving behind the student council office, Wataru walked quickly along the halls that were now quiet during class. While he was walking, tears sprang to his eyes and this time he didn't bother to try to stifle them.

"A laughable kiss… What the hell is that…?" Wataru murmured, shedding tears. "Your sense of humor totally sucks…" As he spoke the falling tears made a drip-drop rhythm that, despite his sadness, seemed funny somehow. He started to laugh through his tears. He would go on crying through his laughter forever.

The rumor died down and everyone soon forgot about it without Wataru really having to do much. Kawamura

showed his mettle and put the moves on Mai again, only to
be dumped again, but he seemed to have quit the drinking and
cursing Yuichi sessions. Instead, he said he wanted to join
the basketball team—even though it was almost the end of
the first semester of their second year—and he actually made
the cut.

Wataru kept his word and tried his best to avoid Yuichi,
and for his part, Yuichi kept his distance from Wataru as well.
According to a new rumor, Yuichi's ring was intact and in
good condition, but Wataru would probably never see the day
when he could confirm that. The thought made his heart ache
with sadness.

Karin was a Cancer, born in July, so there was still plenty
of time before her actual birthday. "But maybe when you
and I are both free, why don't we…?" And that was how she
compelled Wataru to go shopping for a present the next day.
What he really wanted to do was spend a quiet day at home,
nursing his broken heart, but he knew that reason wouldn't fly
with Karin.

"You can't stay depressed, you've got to find new love!" she
said as she chased him out of the house. "Oh, this is the place.
I found it on the internet. It said that all their accessories are
originals! Isn't it cute?!"

"Don't pick something that too expensive."

Completely ignoring Wataru's remark, as soon as they
entered the store, Karin's eyes darted like a hunter's. Ever
since that ring, Wataru had been shunning all accessories, but
there were plenty of classy unisex designs that seemed like his
style, so he started to think about buying something.

"Huh? Do you want something too, Wataru?"

"I'm thinking about it, if there's something good."

"Well, that's a step in the right direction! This week, you
looked like you were going to die! But now your spirit has
bounced back a bit. That's a sign you're coming around.

Hurray!"

"You're exaggerating." In truth, the pain in his heart hadn't healed at all. Every day he had to chase away the vestiges of Yuichi's memory, but he didn't want to get into that conversation with her.

Falling in love had happened so fast, but love required what seemed like a lifetime to figure out. Wataru was tormented by this illogical principle.

"Welcome." She must have heard them come in, because a young woman came out from the back. He had the feeling that within the store was a metal-working studio. She may have been working on something because she wore an apron and took off the army gloves she had been wearing as she greeted them cheerfully. "If there's anything that interests you, I can take it out. Please feel free to ask."

"These are all made here, right? You design them yourself?" Karin inquired in a friendly voice, and the woman nodded slightly. She said that she was still an apprentice and that she worked at the store part-time while she was in school. The owner created almost all the merchandise herself, and then she started raving about her.

"Oh, here she is. That's the owner." The woman pointed at the door and both Wataru and Karin turned. A beautiful woman dressed elegantly in a simple silk blouse and matching linen pants came in carrying cardboard boxes with both hands.

"What...?" As soon as Wataru saw her face, he was rooted to the spot. The woman who had just been introduced as the owner was the very same beauty whom Yuichi had called Toko.

Toko smiled at them in greeting and as the part-time girl helped her, they disappeared into the back. After a moment Toko came back out alone. The young woman who had come out before must have taken her work up again. Smiling gracefully just as she had when she was with Yuichi, Toko began to explain the pieces to Karin.

"That's right. Now it's all about silver and gold. There are a lot of silver bangles out, but I'm not sure that's your style... Since it's your birthday, why don't you let your boyfriend spoil you a bit and get something like a ring?"

"No, unfortunately, he's not my boyfriend." Karin hastened to wave her hands, denying what Toko said. That was what made Toko look from Karin to Wataru for the first time.

Of course, there was no reason to think that Toko would recognize Wataru but nevertheless his heart began to pound. Since Toko was Wataru's rival in love in a way, it took some effort for him to maintain his composure.

"Excuse me," she said. "Are you a student at Ryokuyo High?"

"Huh...? Yes, but..."

"Then do you know a third-year student named Yuichi Kazuki? I'm his cousin."

So she is a relative... he said to himself, while all he could do was nod vaguely. Whether she was a first cousin or second cousin, she was still in much more likely to be his love interest than a guy like he was.

It seemed that his restrained response was unsatisfactory for Karin. She quickly cut into their conversation, "We know Kazuki very well!" she emphasized. "He's helped my brother out many times. He was...a really great guy."

"Karin, you're using the past tense."

"Oh, whoops... But, as far as you're concerned, Wataru, he is as good as dea-... I'm so sorry." Mistakenly, Karin had forgotten that Toko was there, and she hurriedly bobbed her head.

But rather than be offended, Toko had knit her perfectly groomed brows together as she said solemnly, "Actually, he is acting like a dead person."

"You mean, Kazuki?"

"Yes. That boy is so proud, and I'm sure he acts perfectly

normal at school, but I'm told he's almost completely stopped speaking at home. He doesn't eat and he won't come out of his room. It seems he's been like this for an entire week."

"A week…" As Toko spoke, Karin casually poked Wataru in the ribs with her elbow. Speaking of this past week, Wataru had been leading nearly the same dark lifestyle as he tried to recover from the shock of his lost love. Could this be pure coincidence?

"I don't know what happened, but his parents are both very worried and they came to discuss it with me. Yuichi's brother is married and lives in another city, but he and I grew up together, so we're like brother and sister…"

"And you don't know the cause?"

"Yuichi won't say a word. Was there anything at school? Some trouble?"

"Trouble…?"

"That kid, ever since he was a child, he's been good with people. But somehow, I think that's caused a lot of stress for him. And because he does so well, people's expectations of him are high, too."

"He's kind, isn't he?" As soon as the words were out of his mouth, Wataru himself was surprised. Yuichi had been cruel to him many times. The only time he showed any kindness was that one time in the library. To be sure, he had seen barely a fragment of his kindness.

But… Wataru searched through his memory. Thinking of the basketball game, Wataru felt suddenly saddened. Yuichi had pretended he was participating on a whim, and with victory right in front of him, as an outsider he had yielded the win to the team. That's Yuichi's true nature, even Wataru could say that with certainty now. He's so proud, he had shrugged it off as being "annoying," but he had waited for Wataru to come out after him. He had felt, instinctively, that Wataru would understand him.

"I can't stand to see him like this." Toko put her hand to her cheek, letting out a troubled sigh. "He's acting like someone who's had his heart broken. For a boy who seems so perfect, I wonder if it didn't work out the way he had hoped. And after all I did to help him…"

"Help?" Unconsciously, Wataru took a step closer to Toko, not willing to let that word get by. Why would someone like Toko, who was already loved by Yuichi, need to help him? It was her ring that Yuichi treasured—"It's precious to me so I don't want to lose it," Wataru had heard him say.

No, wait a minute… Just then, a piece fell into place in Wataru's mind.

"A friend made that for me and… it's precious to me and I don't want to lose it." *A friend made it for him…* ***"It was a lot to ask, but I had Toko make it for me as a gift."***

Could it be that…she was the one who made that ring…at Kazuki's request?

"The same ring worn by the person he loves. That's what he asked me to make."

"The person he loves…"

"Yes. All I know is that it's someone at his school."

"Wh-When was that?"

"Umm… I think it was around the time the cherry blossoms starting falling, so it must have been in April. You know, there's a line of cherry trees from the station all the way to Ryokuyo High, right? He asked me right after we had gone to see them. So it probably was…"

"April…" That was about the same time that Wataru had first lost his ring. He didn't know where it was for about a week, and then one day it just reappeared all of a sudden. Could it be that Yuichi was somehow involved with that?

He didn't know. Toko had said that she didn't know anything about the other person. And besides, Wataru had bought that ring at some random store. It was probably all about someone else's ring. And anyway, Yuichi's attitude towards him had never given him reason to think otherwise.

Rather, hadn't Wataru been bothered that Yuichi seemed to hate him so much? That had made him sad, which was why he had lashed out at him so many times, while Yuichi would just calmly take it.

But wait, wasn't Yuichi supposed to be a stubborn, proud guy?

"Are you in love with me?" In Wataru's imagination, Yuichi said this with a slightly wicked smile. Now he wanted to ask the same question himself. Facing that handsome, roguish face, he wanted to ask him right away.

Are you in love with me…?

"Um, uh… Excuse me, do you know where Kazuki is today? Please tell me."

"Huh?"

"I want to see him! There's something I have to ask him about in person. And it has to be now!"

"Y-Yuichi? He's probably at home…but I've heard he's cooped up in his room, so…" Perhaps overwhelmed by Wataru's urgency, Toko answered seeming somewhat frightened. Karin, who had no idea what was going on, looked with astonishment at her suddenly lively brother.

"Home? The shortcut is through the playground, right?"

"Y-Yes… How did you know?"

"Thank you very much!" He bowed his head briskly and rushed out of the store, leaving Karin behind.

"Wataru…?!" *What about my present…?* She refrained from continuing, as she looked at Toko next to her, who was just as stunned. "How long have you known?"

"Huh?"

"About Wataru. If you didn't know him, you wouldn't have known where he goes to school just by looking at his face. And you wouldn't have talked about such a private matter so openly, not usually anyway."

"My, you're an intelligent one." Toko's shoulders shook with a giggle as she peered into Karin's unyielding eyes. "You look exactly like your brother. I wonder why Yuichi didn't choose you. Then there wouldn't have been any obstacles. He could have professed his feelings, and you'd be together. There'd be no need for such a hopeless crush."

"But, if he was only interested in looks, then he wouldn't have fallen in love with Wataru, a guy, in the first place, right? Kazuki looks cool, but isn't he a hopeless romantic? There was that ring, and the fact that he's taken a fancy to Wataru…"

"Wataru's cute. He has a nice face, but he seems so intense. For an honor student like Yuichi, someone hotheaded like your brother is the perfect match," Toko said keenly, then she brought her face close to Karin's mischievously. "Yuichi, he has a photo of your brother. It's a snapshot from a school festival or something. I happened to see that he was secretly hiding it. So when Wataru came into the store today, it all clicked. I thought, Oh, I see, my little Yuichi was done in by this boy."

"So…does that bother you?"

"What? No, I'm just surprised." Toko shook her head quietly, smiling. "If Yuichi becomes even more manly through his love for Wataru, then I have no complaints. I love to admire him and show him off, you know…" They both laughed.

"So let's pick out your present then, at your brother's expense, of course," Toko said, courteously taking out the key to the showcase. "Go on and pick something expensive, that's the least he can do. For someone standing at the peak of happiness, it's an obligation… Don't you think?"

On his way to the park, the sun was beginning to set. Consumed with anxiety, Wataru instinctively quickened his pace and hurried on. If possible, he wanted to see Yuichi's face in the daylight, and if the gods favored this match he would still have plenty of time. That was his hope as he walked on silently under the indigo sky.

Passing by the water fountain and cutting along the jungle gym where the girl had been playing, Wataru continued. Across the way should be Yuichi's house, where the large hydrangea bushes were in full bloom.

And then.

"That's the wrong way.   Where do you think you're going?"

"Huh?"

"My house is three doors down from the one with the hydrangeas.   That one is the widow, Mrs. Kanazawa's.   Got it?"

"Kazuki…" There was a mountain of questions he wanted to ask—"Why are you here?" or "Since when?"—but just seeing Yuichi's face made everything better, he looked so wonderful as he appeared from the shadows of the hydrangeas.

Wataru stopped, breathing slowing and deeply as he waited for him to approach. What would he say first? If he took back what he had said last week about being through with him, Yuichi would probably smile and forgive him. As he thought about it though, he began to lose confidence, and without thinking he closed his eyes.

Preparing for what was about to happen, the moment he tried to take a deep breath, Wataru was overtaken by Yuichi's lips. Falling under his sweet breath, the slight fever emanated from their mingled mouths and began to spread throughout Wataru's body.

Shifting the angle of his head and alternating between soft and deep kisses, Wataru found himself tightly embraced by Yuichi.   Something about the way that his arms wrapped around his back, warming him like the sun, brought back memories.

Their warm tongues entwined, and as they pressed their lips together again and again, each of them passionately savored the other's breath.   Wataru kept his eyes closed from the

dizziness, and so it seemed as if Yuichi's warmth and kisses were his whole world.

After their lips finally parted, they remained in each other's arms for a while, listening to each other's heartbeat. If either of them had tried to speak, the indiscreet sound would have shattered the moment, so it seemed they were both helpless in the silence.

Before long, though, Yuichi hesitantly broke the spell. In a rather hoarse voice, he lovingly pronounced Wataru's name. "Wataru…"

"Yeah."

"Do you…love me?"

"Yeah."

"I see." That was all Yuichi said before falling silent again. Instead of confessing himself, he tightened his embrace, and Wataru gave a long sigh.

"Toko called me. When she said you were on your way over here, for a second, I honestly thought you were coming to punch my lights out."

"Why would I come to fight with you?! You're so rude!"

"There was an actual battle on my birthday, you know. Because of the weird rumor you started, girls came down in droves, all bearing gifts and wanting to know the truth. But none of them knew what your sister looked like, so they all suspected each other. In the end, it was a huge mess."

"So that's what happened…?" That must have been why Yuichi had been so irritated in the student council office. Because of the careless rumor, all of his efforts to be polite to the girls had gone to waste, so it was no wonder his attitude had been so reckless.

"I've decided I'm never going to be polite to girls again, no matter what. I'll stop being kind to them, too."

"A-Are you sure? You know, your reputation will suffer…"

"Who cares? Never mind that, you'd better be careful yourself. In the first place, acting like a cheap marriage con artist, don't get yourself engaged so easily… Man, you piss me off."

"Engaged?! T-To who?!" Hearing this nonsense Wataru suddenly got upset again.

Yuichi loosened his arms and released Wataru, slowly sticking his hand in the pocket of his parka. "I'm used to having girls cry on me, but this time even I didn't know what to do. You'd better apologize to Takako later yourself."

"Takako? Who's that?"

"My cute little niece. Takako Kazuki, five years old. Here," he said curtly, as the ring that Wataru thought he had thrown away appeared in his outstretched palm.

"Wh-Why…?"

"I got it back for you. I couldn't stand it if you got engaged without my consent. She was here on my birthday. With my brother."

As he listened to Yuichi, Wataru remembered his exchange with the young girl on the jungle gym. With her pink dress and ribbons in her hair, the little one had really believed that Wataru had given her a wedding ring. "Miniature long-haired dachshund…"

"You mean Puru? That damn dog, during the girlfight, he managed to escape. Then I got to spend the rest of my birthday looking all over for him." As if the memory exasperated him, the furrow between Yuichi's brows grew even deeper.

Wataru smiled bitterly as he took the ring and cautiously tried to ask the question that he had thought about on his way over. "Uh, umm… When I lost my ring that time, was it you who put it back on my desk? If it was, then why did you pretend not to know about it when I told you?"

"Toko told you everything, didn't she? You sure have a mean streak. So cruel…" What Yuichi said was very unfair, but Wataru calmly waited for an answer, looking up at the evening sky as he began to lose patience at last.

"…It was a total coincidence that I found the ring. Of

course, I had no idea who the owner was, and to be honest, I didn't really care either. Then, two or three days later, I was killing time in the student council office looking through photo albums when I found a snapshot of you at the school festival. In the photo, you were wearing the ring that I'd found. But, it's a generic ring, it could have been anyone's, right? Since I didn't know for sure, I secretly put it on your desk to see how you'd react."

"S-So…you were nearby? When I found the ring?" Wataru's voice rose in surprise, as Yuichi shrugged his shoulders without remorse.

"Pretty close. I stood in the doorway to watch your reaction. At the time, I treated it like a kind of game, so if I was wrong, then that was that."

"So, that's how…"

"But you were happy."

That's what I was going to say, Wataru was about to reply. But he didn't say a word when he saw the sincere look in Yuichi's eyes.

"When you saw the ring, you looked wonderful. Your eyes sparkled, and your whole face broke into a smile. I'd never seen a smile like that before. It was at that moment that I fell in love with you."

"……"

"The second time, of course, I panicked. I just happened to be using the third floor fountain, and of all the people to lend my handkerchief to, it turned out to be you. Do you have any idea how awkward I felt? I was wearing the ring I copied from you. My only thought was that I couldn't let you see. You have no idea how rough it was after that to have to talk to you."

"Why? If you'd just told me honestly…"

"Another guy suddenly confesses his love for you, and you'd say OK, just like that? I was struggling with my own feelings, too. I never imagined that I'd find myself in love with a younger man..." At that point, Yuichi's face blushed. His formerly cold eyes glistened warmly, and there in front of Wataru's eyes was the guy he loved. For the first time, here was the real Yuichi Kazuki.

"Kazuki..."

"That's nice. I finally got to see it."

"Huh?"

"That same smile. It's the smile I fell in love with. I thought I'd probably never get to see it again. Since I never even dreamed that it would become mutual between us."

"Why not?"

"C'mon, Wataru, could you go up to someone you don't know and say, 'I'm in love with you and I copied your ring. So, would you go out with me?' I'm sorry, but that's too much. Even if I am the stud of the century, it's just impossible."

"Oh, really..." Wataru had been listening intently but when he heard this ridiculous comment, he broke off the conversation randomly. *Whatever,* he sighed, trying to slip the ring onto his middle finger. "Huh?"

"What?"

"It doesn't fit... Why not? Why doesn't it fit?! This last week I should've lost weight, and you're telling me I gained it?!"

"Oh, that won't fit your middle finger." Yuichi flatly answered Wataru, who was all worked up beside him. "That one's mine."

"You said... mine..."

"I've got your ring. Usually, you can tell by looking. The sizes are different."

"W-Wh-Why...?"

"You love me, don't you?"

"Huh?"

"Then it follows that the position of our rings should change, right? Think about it, Wataru. Both of our rings fit the *other's* ring finger, right? Then it's logical for us to exchange them, don't you agree?" Putting Wataru's ring on his right ring finger, Yuichi's eyes twinkled like he had been caught in the middle of a trick.

After a moment, Wataru noticed this with surprise, as he cracked a brief bitter smile, and slipped Yuichi's ring onto his own ring finger.

Starting tomorrow, a new rumor would fly through the school. They could already see everyone making a fuss about Yuichi's ring moving from his middle finger, and Wataru getting his matching ring back.

But in the end, only the ring fingers know the truth.

The Lonely Ring Finger

Wataru Fujii turned pale when he saw the numbers flash before his eyes. "Damn! *Double* damn! I was supposed to be there half-an-hour ago!"

Wataru's new wristwatch was one of those popular, cyber-digital styles. He had been excited when he bought it, but his boyfriend, Yuichi Kazuki, had only smiled cryptically without really saying much. Now, after being kept waiting for so long, he was sure to make a sarcastic remark like, "What's the point of having such a huge display dial?" Wataru's trot broke into a run and, almost without stopping, he burst into the coffee shop where they were meeting.

But then.

"…Wataru. What's the point of the display dial on your watch?"

"I know…"

"You're more than half an hour late…and all you can say is, 'I know'?" Resting his arm on the back of his chair, Yuichi threw a chilly glare back at him. As usual, he wore a calm, collected expression, but his anger was clearly conveyed by the coldness of his look. This wasn't surprising. Because of final exams before the impending summer vacation, it had been several days since they had actually had a chance to meet, just the two of them.

"Sorry, Kazuki. Just as I was leaving class, I got caught by my homeroom teacher, and the conversation just went on and on… I ran to get here, but…"

"I can tell that just by looking at you."

Sure enough, Yuichi didn't want to listen to his excuses.

Trying to catch his breath, Wataru sat down across from him, but when he saw the empty glass in front of Yuichi, he slumped even more. "I said I was sorry…"

"It's okay, but you'd better order something. The owner has been waiting impatiently for a while."

"Uh, right. Do you want anything else, Kazuki? My treat to make up for it."

"Don't think you can act like an old man and try to bargain with me. I already ordered another iced coffee. Is that okay for you, too?"

"Oh, sure…" He nodded hesitantly as Yuichi quickly turned to the old man at the counter to add Wataru's order. The softness of his voice and his demeanor was instantly so mild it was as if he were another person. There really was no reason for him to be treated differently, and without realizing it Wataru began to get annoyed. It's true that he had been late (which was bad) but seeing as how he was his boyfriend, he thought he could expect somewhat special treatment. However, it seemed that in the two months they had known each other, there were an overwhelming number of times when Yuichi had been particularly unkind. Why was it that the honor student who was trusted by everyone became a tyrant when it came to Wataru? Of course, Yuichi wasn't acting recklessly just to hurt Wataru's feelings, but nevertheless he found Yuichi's discretion toward the old man provoking.

"Why did your homeroom teacher stop you?"

By the time they both had their iced coffees, the warmth had already returned to Yuichi's eyes. But that made no difference to Wataru. Unlike Yuichi, who had excellent grades, you couldn't say that he was a brain. Wataru made such a face that Yuichi could already guess the answer to his question.

"Judging from your silence, I'd say your grades must have slipped."

"…Bingo. But I wouldn't say they've *all* slipped, only English, classical Japanese, history, social studies…"

"That's most of them, isn't it? Wataru, you're really having a hard time. And after I told you what to study..."

"There's no way I could remember everything you told me to study! Well, on the other hand, I improved in math and physics, didn't I? Anyway, I don't have to worry about the university entrance exams until next year. From now on, I'll try harder."

"Entrance exams..."

"Speaking of which, it's much worse for you than for me, isn't it? Did you already decide what university you want to go to?" It was all he could come up with as he tried his best to shift the subject from his own grades. But unexpectedly, Kazuki's expression stiffened as he smiled and silently thought of an answer.

Wataru grew uneasy again as Yuichi made no effort to speak. "What's the matter...? Did I say something wrong?"

"No, it's nothing." Quickly covering up with a smile, Yuichi slowly reached his left hand out for the glass. He did seem to be hung up on something, but Wataru couldn't bring himself to pry any further. Whatever he might have said, he probably had been a little insensitive since Yuichi *was* studying for his exams. While Wataru went over this in his mind, suddenly Yuichi murmured, "Soft-serve ice cream..."

"Huh? Did you say, 'soft-serve ice cream'?"

"I just remembered now. Wataru, you have a sweet tooth, don't you? Toko told me about this totally delicious soft-serve ice cream place that's in Nishi-Ogikubo. Why don't we go there some time?"

"Seriously? Nishi-Ogi's pretty close, isn't it?!"

"Once I've finished with these exams, why don't we have a proper date?" There was a strange forcefulness to Yuichi's words, but Wataru wholly agreed with him.

The guy who was known for his looks throughout their school—not to mention the entire school district—was dating another guy who was a year younger than he was. If that fact were out in the open, it would surely start a riot. As it was, Yuichi was already the center of everyone's—especially the girls'—attention. Because of that fact, even though their feelings were mutual, in reality the two of them couldn't go out on real dates. Even the coffee shop where they met today was just some little place where the old couple who ran it barely scraped by. It wasn't the kind of place any other students would frequent, which was why they felt they could meet here on their way home without having to worry.

"We'd better get going," Yuichi said and Wataru rushed to grab the bill. He may have called him an old man who wanted to bargain, but Wataru intended to pay today. He did mean it as an apology for being late, and since already two out of three times Yuichi had quickly taken care of the check, it would look bad if he didn't treat for a change. Unaware of Wataru's feelings, though, Yuichi tried to steal the bill from him.

"What are you doing, Wataru? Give me that."

"I said it's on me today. Kazuki, you always pay."

"C'mon, it's not very much. Don't worry about it, hurry up and hand it over."

"Why are you ordering me around?!"

"You're more like an old woman than an old man, bickering with me about who pays the bill!"

"I'm only 17!"

Shrugging off the pointless argument, Wataru forcefully brought the bill up to the cashier. But when she totaled it up, Wataru noticed that the amount seemed like more than he had expected. Thinking it would rude to ask the old lady at the register had lost her marbles, he cautiously inquired, "Excuse me, uh… It was three iced coffees…"

"No. Doesn't the receipt say it's for four?"

"Yes, b-but I had one and he had two."

"Ah… That young student over there, he's been here for more than an hour. So before you arrived, I'd already brought him two iced coffees."

"A-A whole hour…?" What the old woman said struck Wataru at the bottom of his heart, and Wataru quickly looked around for Yuichi. He had thought he was behind him, but he was already heading out of the café with a look like he had swallowed bitterness.

"He was waiting that long…?"

"That young man, I don't how many times he eagerly looked at the clock. You two must be quite good friends."

"……"

Wataru hurried to pay and, bowing his head with a single nod, he rushed out of the coffee shop. Against the backdrop of the just-darkening sky, he could see Yuichi's lovely silhouette—his handsome form and his small head like a model's. But Wataru could also detect a trace of sulkiness that was out-of-place with his mature looks.

As if Wataru had snuck a peek at his awkwardness, Yuichi said somewhat defiantly, "That's why I said I'd pay. You're always…"

"Kazuki…"

"Don't get the wrong idea. My homeroom ended a little early. That's all, nothing more…"

Perhaps that was true. Either way, though, Wataru was touched. The fact that Yuichi had been looking forward to their long-awaited meeting was enough to make him happy. *Kazuki was just as excited as I was…*

The thought warmed Wataru's heart. When he had unluckily got snared by his homeroom teacher, all he could think about was Yuichi's face. His mind had raced as he wondered how they would spend the little time they had together, and he had hardly paid any attention to the teacher's lecture. It was unusual for him, but no one was happier than he was.

At that moment, Kazuki was probably thinking the same thing… Wataru was sure that until he had burst into the coffee shop and Yuichi had given him that chilly glance, he had probably had on a sweet smile. Just picturing that look,

Wataru's own face bloomed into a grin.

"Hey, what are you mooning about to yourself?" Yuichi said spitefully, with a frankly distasteful expression. But Wataru didn't mind. He caught up to his side and cheerfully held out his right hand. Yuichi seemed to blink at the sudden movement, saying, "…What?!" as he looked back and forth from Wataru to his hand.

Wataru smiled again, closing the distance between them as he lowered his voice a little. "Let's walk hand in hand, just for a little bit? There's hardly anyone around now."

"Huh…"

"It's all right. It's only about fifty meters until we get to the main road."

"You seem like you're in a good mood all of a sudden… really." His words sounded weary but his left hand grasped Wataru's without hesitation.

Wataru's now-heavy palm was held with a gentle strength and against his skin he could feel the cool ring Yuichi was wearing on his ring finger.

That's right, Wataru said softly in his mind. The paired ring he had exchanged with Yuichi was also settled on his own finger. As long as this ring continued to sparkle on each other's hands, Yuichi would always be by his side. There was absolutely no need for him to get pissed about details like the look in his eye or the tone of his voice.

"Well, soon it will be summer vacation. I can't wait!"

"Do you have plans to travel anywhere?"

"No, of course not. Why would you ask something crazy like that? Won't you and I be hanging out every day, away from everyone's attention? I mean, since we can never be alone together during school."

"Uh… well…"

Was it his imagination, or did Yuichi's belated reply sound totally monotone? But Wataru had been so carried away with holding hands and talk of summer vacation that he hardly paid any attention. Unfortunately, he also didn't notice the fact that Yuichi's profile had grown slightly darker.

"...Prep school?   You mean, for the entire summer vacation?"

It was the last weekend of the first school term, and Wataru and Yuichi were meeting up again for a date at Nishi-Ogikubo station. They had planned to go to the soft-serve ice cream shop that they had talked about the other day, and until now Wataru had been casually relaying a conversation from dinner the night before. But his mood abruptly shifted when he heard Yuichi's words.

"Really, I tried to tell you when we saw each other before... I'm sorry."

"Is that so?"

"Since I'm trying to get into Tokyo University, my summer schedule has to be adjusted for the exams. And since my parents have already paid the tuition, I can't really skip-out and run around with you. So...if you and I had been going out before prep school was decided, we could have had a bit more time."

At some point they had both stopped walking and were now standing in the middle of the street. Yuichi may not have been aware, because all he could do was stare at Wataru apologetically. If the car horns hadn't prodded them along, he might have kept standing there with his head bowed deeply. His expression was so downcast that even his beautiful eyes were cast in shadow.

Moving out of the way to the side of the road, they looked at each other again. Wataru was surprised by what Yuichi had said, but he was more concerned about his poor spirits.

"Well, it must be a pretty popular class if you've had a reservation for this long."

"Yeah, it's been filled to-capacity since six months ago."

"Well then, I think you really ought to go. And there aren't classes on the weekend, are there? That way, at least we could still see each other once a week, right?"

"Well... at least..." Yuichi nodded reluctantly as Wataru's black eyes brightened and he heaved a sigh of relief.

"Your voice had gotten so serious all of a sudden, I thought you meant that we wouldn't see each other at all. That wouldn't be fair."

"Wouldn't be fair? You..."

"I'm not a little kid! Are you saying that you won't be able to hang out at all during summer vacation? I don't want to be responsible for you failing the exams. Why don't we think about how we can make time to see each other?"

"...I'm surprised. You're being so optimistic."

"I've heard the girls in my class who go out with third-years complain a lot. They say it's really hard to date someone who's studying for the exams. But next year, *I'll* be the one taking them. And then I'll really have something to worry about."

That truly was how Wataru felt. With Kazuki's grades, he could expect to get in anywhere easily, but that wasn't the case for Wataru. Next year at this time, he probably wouldn't be thinking about summer vacation either.

Really though, I had hoped to have made some memories to share with Kazuki before then. But saying any of this to Yuichi now would only make him feel worse. Wataru raised his head again to face Yuichi, who still looked uneasy, and good-naturedly patted his left shoulder several times. "It's fine. Instead, can we make a date for every weekend? Promise?"

"Wataru, is that really okay? Are you sure?"

"Uh-huh. But the ice cream today will be your treat. Then I'll forgive you."

"Really...?" Yuichi finally looked relieved and he gave a short sigh. "I'm so glad that you understand. I didn't know what I was going to do if you'd sulked."

"Would I do that? I don't want to pull your leg anymore."

"Anymore… Wait, what do you mean?"

"Didn't you say, Kazuki, that you were never going to be polite to women again, no matter what?"

"Huh…?"

"Well, as a result, you've made a lot of girls cry. I've seen it plenty of times with my own eyes."

"Wataru…" Perhaps Yuichi was reminded of all those incidents, and he faltered in his own response. He had tried his best to deflect girls by coolly rejecting their letters and presents on the spot, smiling and being overly kind. Now that he wore a ring on his left ring finger, he sent many girls away by assuring them with a cold attitude that he was seeing someone, but there were some who didn't give up so easily. The worst were the girls who tried to persuade him with their tears.

"Kazuki, you get this really troubled look on your face, and aren't there girls who get offended that you don't want to go out with them? Who ask you if they're prettier than the person you're dating…?"

"It doesn't matter, I'm used to that."

"Well, it bothers me. I feel bad enough that you've already got such a burden to worry about. It pisses me off when I hear them complaining, 'Kazuki isn't nice anymore.' I feel like the least I can do to make up for it is to support you with your exams."

"……"

"Uh, I-I'm sorry… Did I say too much?"

Yuichi had fallen silent with a pensive look on his face, so Wataru hastened to bring his voice back to normal. He was strangely self-conscious about unintentionally getting so worked-up while he had been talking. He really did feel inferior to Yuichi, but he hadn't meant to complain.

"Now that we've agreed about summer vacation, why don't we change the subject? I can't wait to try this soft-serve ice cream today. Karin really wanted me to bring her along. I'm not kidding. That girl, she sure does pry into what's going on between us!"

"What's going on? What does she think?!"

"What... No, I mean... Look..."

"What?"

"Well... It's just...nothing. She wanted to know how far, you know."

"Oh, I see... Well, well."

He was trying so hard to seem serious, but suddenly Wataru felt like running away. Why was it that their conversation was so off-kilter today? This made him wish that things could be like they were before. By before, he meant...

"Well, you know, all you and I have ever done is kiss."

"K-Kazuki! What do you mean by that?!"

"It's true, isn't it? Maybe that's what Karin expects. She's been watching the progress of our relationship all along; it's almost her right to know."

"To know...what?" He hadn't told Karin anything like that.

Wataru would have argued with him, but it wasn't the kind of thing to talk about in public in the middle of the day, so he shut up. When he thought about it, two male high school students standing on the side of the road passionately talking did present a rather odd picture. In their case, the fact that they weren't lazily crouching with a cell phone in one hand set them apart from other high school students. But however one looked at the wholesome Wataru and Yuichi, with his orderly features that were anything but common, the two would stand out among their surroundings no matter what.

"Chocolate and vanilla..." Yuichi said suddenly after the silence had gone on for a moment. "Which do you like?"

"What?"

"Soft-serve ice cream. This place only has two flavors."

"Ch-Chocolate and vanilla, that's all...?" Taken aback by

the abrupt question, Wataru mulled it over, then mumbled shyly, "Chocolate, I guess." He went on, "Vanilla is so basic, I always get tired of it halfway through."

"Then I'll have vanilla. That way, we can each have half and neither will get bored, right?"

"……"

"You don't want to? I guess you're not a kid. That's not enough to make you feel better."

"Feel better… Me?"

"What's with you today? You're going through the whole range of emotions. And anyway, that talk about the kiss was as shocking to you as the part about summer vacation, wasn't it? Why would I think that soft-serve was going to cheer you up?" As Yuichi spoke, he smiled with a sort of sad and discouraged look.

The next moment, Wataru shook his head vigorously, shattering the heavy mood that had enveloped them. "But, I…"

"Hmm?"

"I have a huge craving for soft-serve ice cream."

"Wataru…"

"Right. I want some right now. Kazuki, let's hurry up. Let's not waste any more time." There was no longer any trace of darkness on Wataru's face as he eagerly walked off. Smiling at his boyfriend, who had bounced back so quickly, Yuichi hurriedly started after him.

They were already counting down to summer vacation. Things certainly were different from how he first expected, but being in love with each other was like the difference between heaven and hell. Whatever the case, now it *really* was summer. He had a boyfriend to kiss and hold hands with, and it didn't matter whether he would only have the chance to see him less than a handful of times; his days would be full. That's right. *It doesn't matter if I can only see him once a week, or if we can't go places on dates. The important thing is that things are good between Kazuki and me...*

Something somewhere in his heart told him this was nothing more than a bluff, but he ignored it for now. There were times when Yuichi was brisk with him, but normally he was very kind. Wataru knew that if he had really been upset and disappointed, Yuichi would surely have withdrawn from prep school. That was exactly the reason why he hadn't acted selfishly and given him a hard time.

"Hey, Kazuki. Can I change my request?"

"What?"

"Will you get me both chocolate *and* vanilla?" Wataru said, looking back as Yuichi beamed at him and nodded.

When we can't meet, we'll keep in contact as much as possible.

Making that promise, Wataru and Yuichi each started their summer vacation. Yuichi went to prep school five days a week, doing his best to gear-up for the exams. It wasn't that he aimed for the challenges, but he was by nature rather serious. Maybe it was because, ever since he was little, he had performed so above-average that those around him placed higher and higher expectations on him. In response, Yuichi now felt obliged.

On the other hand, since Wataru didn't even have a part-time job, his days were pretty relaxed. Today he had gone with his best friend Kawamura to see the horror movie everyone was talking about, and now they had stopped to try the new fast food burger joint.

"But, is that really your excuse, Wataru?"

"I have no choice, do I? The best thing I can do is to stay out of his way."

"Hmm... You seem weirdly understanding of this whole thing." Leaning back in his chair heavily, Kawamura seemed impressed. For him, a guy who lived for love, it didn't seem possible that he would understand Wataru's rationality. Biting into the hamburger in his right hand, he made a peevish face and said, "What's *up* with that?"

He went on. "If it were me, I would have complained straight-off. I mean, it's summer, right? Aren't the exams next year?"

"C'mon, think about it. Kazuki's had all kinds of trouble since we've been together."

"By trouble, do you mean that finally girls aren't as interested in him? But that's to be expected. Who would go after him now that he's wearing a ring on his left ring finger? And then, for you, wasn't it such a hassle when everyone wanted to know all about the whole ring incident? It goes both ways, doesn't it?"

By now, it had been established that the fact that their rings matched was a coincidence. But there were still girls who pestered Wataru with the tenacity of television reporters. And since they had both started wearing their rings on the left ring finger, now they eyed him suspiciously and asked, with all seriousness, "Maybe you two are a couple?"

"It's just that since Kazuki's attitude has suddenly grown cold, the girls have also gotten quieter…" He really didn't want to think about it, but Wataru took a good look at recent events. "That's the reason why Kazuki's reputation has suffered. It's like somehow he's the bad guy."

"As long as he said it was okay, you've got no reason to feel guilty. And now that it's mutual, you can't have any fun if all you do is hold yourself back."

"I don't do that." That was the only part that Wataru flatly denied. "Just thinking about Kazuki makes me happy. I've never felt this way about any of the girls I've dated. So…if I can't see him for a little while, I can handle it."

"You're not telling me you're *in love*?"

"No, I'm serious. I mean, my heart beats too fast, there are times when I lose control. Isn't Kazuki good-looking? How one person can have so many facial expressions…"

"When you're done talking, I'm gonna start calling you two 'stupid couple,'" Kawamura interrupted, seeming bored. This annoyed Wataru since he had been the one fishing for information, but because Kawamura was currently single and on-the-move, it wasn't a subject that interested him. As he reached out for the fries spilled in front of him, he tried to change the subject.

"What about you?"

As expected, he got a frown of disapproval in return. "Unfortunately, it's bad. I found a cool girl in the first-year class but…"

"Hey, you've finally given up on Tachibana! So, what kind of girl is she?"

"Why would a homo like you care?"

"How can you be so obnoxious?!"

"Her name is Miho Ookusa. She's really cute, and she's popular. It's just…too bad I've got no chance. For some reason, they say she hates all guys. Really, she's as pretty as any celebrity, but just by what I've heard, she's slain dozens of guys. Seriously, I'm at a total loss. You could say she's the female version of Yuichi Kazuki."

Once again ticked-off by what he said, Wataru angrily crammed his mouth full of fries. Maybe since Kawamura had seen everything from the very beginning, Wataru would have to tolerate his surprise at his feelings of love. But Kawamura was probably envious that his best friend had found happiness in one shot, and had to tease him about it. And since Kawamura had once considered Yuichi a rival in love, his state of mind must have been rather complex.

Finishing what was left of his hamburger, Kawamura leaned away from the table and whispered, "…So, how far have you guys gone then?"

"*That* again? How many times do I have to tell you, none of your business!"

"Uh-huh. That must mean you've stopped at kissing. Hey,

what have you been doing all this time?"

"Shut up! This isn't the kind of thing you can measure by time!" That really was how Wataru felt in the bottom of his heart, so no matter how much Kawamura baited him, it really didn't bother him. Of course, it wasn't that he wasn't concerned, but since both he and Yuichi were guys there were quite a lot of unknowns when he started to think about it. That was why he had decided that all he could do was let things happen naturally.

"I wonder if such an indifferent attitude is the way to go," Kawamura said in a grumbling tone, almost as if it was on Yuichi's behalf. "Maybe you acted too unconcerned about summer vacation. Do you really love Kazuki?"

"D-Don't ask such rude questions! If I didn't love him, do you think I'd..."

"Huh?"

"I'd get this excited...?" As soon as the words were out of his mouth, his left ring finger grew hot. The ring he had exchanged with Yuichi was glimmering slightly, as if winking at him. Even when they were apart he didn't worry, and it was probably because of the ring.

Finally Kawamura seemed to get tired of teasing him, and he started talking about Miho Ookusa again. Only halfway-listening to him, Wataru lightly rubbed his ring with his fingertip. *I didn't mean to be... indifferent, but...* What if Yuichi felt the same way? He wondered when he would be able to see him next as he flipped through the memo book in his mind.

The sky had been gloomy all day since morning. Thick rain clouds piled up, and the color of the sky was unsettling. To make things even more unpleasant, a damp, warm wind was blowing. The moment Wataru stepped out the door, his sweet features completely fell.

"We should probably change the meeting place..."

Lately they had been using the playground where they had first kissed. Since it was close to Yuichi's house, the standard had become that they would then go to Yuichi's room. At first Yuichi had half-heartedly complained, saying that they weren't schoolchildren, but since Wataru didn't want to waste their time going off elsewhere, he hadn't said anything more. And when they passed by the hydrangeas where their relationship had completely changed, they both squeezed each other's hands. Wataru loved that awkward feeling.

But unfortunately, there wasn't an appropriate place in the park that was protected from the rain. He tried calling Yuichi on his cell phone, but it seemed like he'd turned it off, so he couldn't get through. "It sucks that it's raining," he thought.

While he was walking, one after another the raindrops had started to make a pattern of dots on the pavement. Opening the umbrella he had brought with him, he headed for his destination almost at a run. Since his house was nearby, Yuichi would probably have enough time to go back and get his own umbrella, but he expected that Yuichi wouldn't have done so. Wataru felt propelled by something as he headed for the park, still running silently.

Even though it was early in the afternoon, because of the rain there was hardly a soul in the park. Passing by the water fountain, Wataru reached the cluster of hydrangeas but, contrary to his expectations, he didn't see Yuichi anywhere and he involuntarily let out a sigh until…

"Wataru. Over here."

"Huh…"

"Under the blue slide. Look."

He let his eyes follow the voice he heard as Yuichi slowly appeared from under the blue slide. But since it seemed like there was barely enough space for him to shelter from the rain, both shoulders of the mint green striped shirt he was wearing were completely soaked. Even so, he didn't seem concerned as Wataru watched him glide over to him and under

the umbrella. Without thinking, Wataru said severely, "Hey, what are you gonna do if you catch a cold?! And why did you turn off your cell phone?"

"Huh...? Oh, I was at prep all morning. Did you call?"

"I did. I was worried that you were stuck waiting here. It would be fine if you had an umbrella, but it would really suck if you didn't. You should've gone back to the house..."

"Hey, why would I do that when someone is waiting for me?" Now it was Yuichi who seemed annoyed. He had hesitated over going back to get an umbrella because he was afraid they would miss each other, and now he didn't think he deserved to be given a hard time. But as for Wataru, he was just worried about Yuichi's well-being. He may have been holding back how much he missed him, but even if there wasn't the obstacle of his exam studies, if Yuichi caught a cold it would ruin everything. Since then it would be his own fault, though, it wouldn't do for Wataru not to be calm about it.

"What do you mean, I'm disappointed in you. Why are you being so rational?" Unaware of Wataru's feelings, Yuichi abruptly averted his gaze. As the rainfall grew stronger and swallowed them up, the silence seemed to bear down on them meaningfully. It had been a whole week since they had seen each other—why did there have to be this awkward feeling? Wataru was dejected by this incredible sadness when, facing his side, Yuichi uttered, "Even if my clothes got a little wet, I thought it was better to meet you earlier."

"......"

"Isn't that right? It's finally the weekend. But I never imagined that you'd start it by lecturing me."

"But, I just..."

"And here I was thinking that you were looking forward to seeing me. That's what I *would* have thought. When I told you that I couldn't see you much during summer vacation, instead of being disappointed, you were rather easily convinced. You've got plenty of other people to spend your time with, don't you? And aren't you the one who keeps your cell phone turned off? Like when you're with Kawamura."

"Wh-What, you sound like a little kid! That was 'cause I was at a movie! You're the one who had his phone off even though we're supposed to meet!" Wataru's voice rose in anger at the unexpected retort.

But even as Yuichi gave him an icy glance, he said meekly, "From now on, I guess I'll pay more attention to my phone when we're meeting."

"Kazuki…"

"I love it when you come running in late. It's written all over your face how much you want to see me. That's the Wataru I fell in love with. I don't want someone who's always attentive and reasonable."

As soon as he heard that, Wataru began to understand what Yuichi was so hung up on. At the same time, he recalled how, the other day, Kawamura had accused him of being too indifferent. Since he loved him and really didn't mind waiting it out, he realized he very well may have given Yuichi the wrong idea. If that was the case, it was quite a shock.

Yuichi may have thought that he had said too much since Wataru kept quiet, so he lightly cleared his throat. But the patter of raindrops on the umbrella discouraged him and he lost the opportunity to say something else. The silence went on for a little longer, however, they couldn't just stand there in the rain forever. Soon Yuichi took a deep breath and patted Wataru on the back as if to prompt him.

"It's no big deal. We' better go inside. There's no reason to stand around in the rain."

"Kazuki…I don't think you understand me."

"What?"

"I was trying to stay out of your way! There had been such a commotion about the ring incident that until now it prevented you from studying, so…the least I could do was try my best to help… That's why!"

While he was talking, he thrust the umbrella he was holding towards Yuichi, who reflexively grasped the handle, leaving Wataru out in the rain.

"Wataru?! You idiot, what are you doing?" Surprised, Yuichi spoke in an unusually flustered voice.

Standing there, Wataru raised his eyes and looked straight at him. His frustration at not being understood and his irritation at not conveying his feelings made his heart ache. But he was reluctant to reveal this, so he kept up his determined attitude.

Yuichi was particularly confused by Wataru's unexpected behavior. Although it was fine for *him* to get wet, he couldn't stand to see his beloved get soaked. Wataru's sudden anger also touched him to the core, the evidence of which was revealed by his remote eyes returning to their normal color. "Wataru… Come back here."

"No! I'm pretty angry, I need to cool off! I'll just get more upset if I see your face."

"Come on…" Because he was usually such a nice guy, Yuichi had completely forgotten about Wataru's stormy side. Exposing himself to the warm summer rain, he looked at Yuichi with his black eyes, wordlessly.

"Do you really think that I like not being able to see you? How can you not understand?! Kazuki, you're smart. How come you don't get it?"

"How am I supposed to know?! With your attitude…"

"My attitude? What do you *mean*, my attitude?"

"I mean… This is totally different from when you're being sweet to me. Now you're always saying, 'We can't waste our time.'"

"What do you mean, *when* I'm sweet to you?! Aren't I always…" Here he broke off.

Impatient with Wataru, who showed no sign of coming back around, Yuichi flung out the umbrella. Catching on the wind, it carved a beautiful arc as if in slow-motion, and for a moment Wataru's gaze was riveted to the sky. Yuichi took that opportunity to stride nearer to him and then he tightly embraced his rain-soaked body. He held him so close that he couldn't speak. Any resistance was pointless.

One time beneath the shade of the same hydrangeas, their bodies had met silently before. Abandoning what he was going to say, Wataru resigned himself to quietly slipping both arms around Yuichi's back. The words he had just swallowed dissolved lightly through his fingertips. No matter how well he chose his words, they would never amount to more than this single embrace. That fact was a little frustrating, but it was impossible to resist this pleasure.

"Kazuki... You sneaky..." All he could do in protest was move his lips. "Why would you do this while you're so angry?"

"I couldn't let you be the only one getting drenched. You're the one who wouldn't come back under the umbrella. And...I shouldn't have said that before. I'm sorry."

"......"

"I really love you, no matter what. Even if you were a better student than I am, I'd still love you."

Wataru didn't even register the absurd example that Yuichi had thrown out. Instead, the sound of him repeating, "I love you" utterly soothed his injured heart. Once again, in a gentle voice that rose above the sound of the falling rain, Yuichi whispered in his ear. "I want to stay like this with you forever. I always want to see you, want to hold you close. I want to know your feelings for me by touching you. That's...honestly and truly how I feel."

"Mmm..." *Me too,* Wataru thought to himself. *Wouldn't it be wonderful if they could forget about reality and just stay here like this?* Looking forward to their first summer together, he had hoped for some special days. When he thought further into the future, he expected to spend many seasons with Yuichi. That was why he could stand to be lonely for a little while, especially when his depression was quickly resolved by being held in his arms like this. Anyway, the rings that had been infused with their feelings glimmered on each other fingers.

Maybe Yuichi knew why he was smiling, because he loosened his arms a bit. As he slowly raised his head, he saw that Yuichi was smiling happily too. The drops falling from his bangs didn't seem to bother him at all, and even soaked from head to toe, he still looked as handsome as ever.

"Wataru…" His voice cracked faintly as he called his name, and Wataru's eyes closed. He cracked a smile at the sign of his approaching lips, but it was an extremely polite kiss. Their moist lips met and their breath mingled. With utmost care, as if he were trying to take in something very fragile, Yuichi's kiss intensified gradually.

Somewhere far off was the sound of the rain. In a corner of his mind, Wataru vaguely registered this while that single kiss transported him to a completely different world. His lips grew numb from the sweet sensation, and the scent of the rain rose up from their wet bodies. Wataru was embraced tightly again, and he murmured, "It's all right," as he was enraptured all over again.

"I'll always love you, Kazuki. Before, you said you wanted to make sure, but what do you need to know? All you ever have to do is ask."

"…It's not words," seeming a little flustered, Yuichi responded hesitantly. "When we don't touch, I start to worry. I'm just like anybody else."

"What do you mean by that?"

"If I ask you something, will you answer me honestly?" Just as he said that, it began to rain harder. He hurriedly picked up the umbrella at their feet and sighed with relief. It was too late to hide behind it, but Wataru regretted that now his face would be covered from the rain. Rumpling his wet bangs with his fingertips, Yuichi looked sexy and instinctively, Wataru was enchanted.

"...So."

"Huh?" While he had been distracted by his face, Wataru had carelessly missed hearing what he had said. Getting a cold glance, he hurriedly apologized. "What did you just say? Do you mind repeating it?"

"Are you testing me? Fine, but only one more time."

"Okay."

"I said, let's go to bed."

As the low mutter reached his ears, next he heard a long sigh.

"Forget it. It sounds stupid the second time."

"Let's go to bed...what? Do you mean...?"

"If you make me say it again, we're through." Maybe because he felt so embarrassed, Yuichi looked at Wataru lightly. His cool, clean-cut good looks seemed to negate the reality of what he said, but "Let's go to bed" echoed in Wataru's ears.

"I know what I said, but it wasn't just out of nowhere." Yuichi spoke again, since Wataru was so surprised he was dumbstruck. "From now on, I'll be able to see you even less. So I didn't think I could wait. It's not just that it would be a relief to do it, but wouldn't it help put my unjustified fears to rest? Then we wouldn't have to have these stupid fights... What do you think, Wataru?"

"Wh-What do I think? It's not so easy... In the first place, if we're talking about wanting to or the timing of it, look, it seems like this is something that should take its own course..."

"But since we have so little time together, how can we do that?"

"Well... I know what you mean, but..." Wataru was at a loss for words at this unexpected development. If he refused, they'd probably get into another argument, but that was no reason to just say, "Okay, let's go to bed!" He didn't know about Yuichi, but he had never been with anyone before.

"Do you not want to?"

"No, it's... I didn't think you would...ask me like that..."
He couldn't draw out his answer forever, so Wataru thought
fast. How could he do this without hurting Yuichi? "Uh...
right. I mean, Kazuki, why don't we make the best of not
seeing each other?"

"Make the best of it? What does that have to do with what
we're talking about?"

"Okay, didn't you say that the national practice exams are in
late September? You said that whether you get into your first
choice ultimately depends on how you do on those. Didn't
you say that's what this summer's prep school is for?"

"Oh..."

"So why don't we wait until the practice exams. Your sense
of accomplishment will be double, and I'll feel like I was
able to support you. Then not seeing each other won't be for
nothing, right? Right?"

Maybe since he had tried so hard to convince him, Yuichi
just looked back at him as if he was overawed. Then he
twisted his mouth and a modest laugh spilled out. Wataru had
no idea why he was laughing, but Yuichi's voice quavered as
he said, "You really don't want to do it, do you?"

"Huh?! No, it's not that I don't want to, that's not it..."

"It's okay. I get it. I was too impatient. Let's do what you
said. There's no point in not making it worthwhile to be apart.
But if it's just to wait until the practice exam is done, that could
have the opposite effect on me... Let's make a condition. If
we add a gamble, then my sense of accomplishment will
triple."

"Like, a bet...?" He didn't think this would happen. Wataru
was again dumbstruck—he just stared at Yuichi, who was still
smiling. They had veered pretty far from what Wataru had
meant by "natural course," but since it had all started with his
own babbling, he really couldn't object now.

"That's right. How about if we say that if I rank in the top thirty on the exams?"

"The top thirty in the whole country?! Don't you think that's a little..."

"If I don't try, I'll never know, will I? Of course, it is a pretty big challenge," he said, but the look on his face wasn't troubled at all. He had no way to know what his chances were by that expression, but no matter how elite a student he was, the top thirty in the country was pretty reckless. Wataru simply couldn't understand why Yuichi would make such an absurd bet.

In the end he had to agree with Yuichi, who had steamrolled his resistance, so they made a new promise. If Yuichi ranked in the top thirty in September, then they would take a step further along in their relationship. Wataru halfway-thought it was ridiculous, but since Yuichi was so into it for some reason, he reluctantly went along.

After the crazy bet, the rest of the summer was a blur.

Wataru still talked on the phone and emailed with Yuichi, but he actually only saw him once after that, and even then, all they did was stand and talk in the park. It was quite a wholesome date. However many times Wataru tried to bring up breaking his promise, he knew Yuichi was really giving it his all so ended up not being able to say anything.

"Don't do yourself in..." Lately, he had started to worry. When his emails would come in at dawn, Wataru was wracked with guilt. He couldn't help but wonder how Yuichi could toil so hard while he coasted through his days.

And that was how summer ended. With a heavy heart, Wataru faced the new school semester while Yuichi was still consumed with studying. Occasionally, Wataru would see him at school, and he would always be carrying a book in one hand. Once again, he offended some of the more superficial girls, but since his popularity was so deeply-rooted, his fierce study habits were soon talked about throughout the school.

Within a single week of the beginning of the term, everyone was certain that Yuichi was aiming for Tokyo University. More and more, Wataru felt that there was no turning back, and his gloom only increased with each day.

"But, why would you go along with a bet like that? I don't get it!"

"Why? I got caught up in the moment, that's all."

"You're idiots, both you and Kazuki."

Wataru had no reply to Kawamura's insult. With each passing day his feelings about the ridiculous promise heightened and, not knowing what else to do, he had tried to talk it over with Kawamura. But his response was just as he'd imagined. Kawamura sat in the coffee shop he had invited him to, with his arms-crossed, drinking the iced café au lait Wataru had paid for. He couldn't fathom why he was still called names when it was *his* treat, but because there was no one else Wataru could turn to, he listened quietly.

"Really, it's totally different from what you said before. If he's acting like it's not something that can be measured by time, then how come the first time you do it is going to be decided by Kazuki's grades?"

"Well, I see what you mean…"

"Since *he* was the one who made the condition, he must be pretty confident." That was the only thing that really seemed to impress Kawamura. He didn't forget to add, "He doesn't just look the part, he even talks like he's running the show. It's creepy."

He went on, "It's not as if he doesn't stand a chance, but top thirty in the country is a big deal. I wonder if he realizes that. Well, whatever, you guys sure are a stupid couple."

"Don't make fun."

"No, I'm serious. This means that Kazuki can't help but study even more, right? And now because he wants to *do it* with you, do you realize the paradox that now your time together decreases even more?"

"Uh..." He was right. Because of that crazy bet, Yuichi needed more time than ever to study, and it had gotten even harder to see him. And, since Wataru was trying his best to be careful not to attract attention, he wouldn't even go over to his class to ask him anything. As a result, chance encounters were the only way that the two of them might see each other. This was the most painful part for the new lovers, who were still in the honeymoon phase of the first two months.

"You guys have got it backwards. What will you do if he really makes it?"

"What do you mean? We made a promise..."

"Oh, so you would do it just like that, without a drop of romance?"

"......"

In truth, Wataru couldn't convince his heart. But since to cancel now would probably seriously dampen Yuichi's enthusiasm, he worried about getting in the way of his studying. It was a no-win situation.

"Man, why did I make that promise..." he whined, falling limply on the table. No matter how much he regretted it, he was already on his way to "doing it within the top thirty!" Neither one of them could do anything to stop it now.

It happened right after gym class ended, three days after he talked to Kawamura.

"Wait a minute..."

"What's the matter, Wataru? If you don't hurry up and change, you'll be late for your next class."

"Hey, Kawamura. Have you seen my ring? I took it off before gym and put it right on top of my towel... Now it's gone. It must have fallen somewhere."

While he was talking, Wataru was already on all fours on the floor. Since hardly anyone was left in the locker room, it was easy to search but, unfortunately, there didn't seem to be anything anywhere that looked like his ring.

"That's weird. It's not like you to lose it by mistake, since you're always so careful with it…"

Since he had already lost it not once but twice, Wataru made an effort to be extremely mindful. Nevertheless, wherever he looked, he could not find his precious ring. And as he went from unsure to quite certain that it was gone, little by little his face drained of color. Kawamura and whoever else was left helped look for it with him, but soon the first bell rang and everyone had to go. Wataru wanted to skip class to keep looking, but since he needed to check in with the ones who had already gone back to class, he had no choice but to give up. Nobody offered the faintest hope about the ring's whereabouts. Even if he had dropped it while changing, the boys' locker room was a closed environment, so it seemed like he should have found it right away. No one had a clue. And since the design matched Yuichi's and had been the talk of the school, everyone said, "Oh, that!" but nothing more.

"Damn… How could it have disappeared…?"

After school he didn't give up, and he walked around the locker room for the hundredth time. He even offered the student on-duty to take care of the room's cleaning himself. But all of his hard work was for nothing.

"Do you think someone just walked off with it?" Kawamura said sympathetically when he came to meet Wataru, bringing him his bag. He had helped him look everywhere, but at the end of the day he could only tilt his head and say in conclusion, "All I can think of is that someone is holding it for you. I mean, doesn't everyone know that it's your ring? If someone took it, they wouldn't be able to wear it, right? People are already talking about Kazuki having a girlfriend, and I've noticed there aren't as many girls who want to wear a paired ring with him. So, isn't wearing it the same as being paired with Kazuki or paired with his girlfriend? Why would someone bother…?"

"But I lost it in the boys' locker room. How would a girl have it?"

"I wasn't talking about a girl. Maybe there's a guy like you, who's lovestruck with Kazuki."

"C'mon, Kawamura." Even though he knew it was an innocent remark, Wataru got angry.

Just as he involuntarily began to pout, there was a light knock on the locker room door. A girl's voice said, "Is someone named Wataru Fujii in there?"

Wataru and Kawamura looked at each other reflexively and both cocked their heads at the same time. It was definitely not the voice of a girl from their class. But who was calling Wataru?

While he hesitated to reply, there was the sound of another knock. Wataru put his hand on the doorknob and yanked the door open. At just the moment that the figure of a girl rushed into view, Kawamura exclaimed behind him.

"Aren't you Miho Ookusa from first-year, 'D' homeroom?"

"Yes, I am." Even though he was overly familiar with her, she nodded and bowed her head without hesitation. Her short hair was cut in a shag just below her ears, and it shined with a healthy gloss as it moved with her. Kawamura seemed rather nervous, and he stammered while Wataru wondered, *Who's Miho Ookusa again...?* As he thought that maybe it was natural since she was so pretty, her name flashed in his memory.

"Oh yeah, you're the female Yuichi Kazuki."

"Excuse me?"

"Oh, sorry. Never mind. Um...Ookusa? Was that you calling me?" He quickly corrected himself, and this time Miho smiled and nodded.

"Yes. I went looking for you in the classroom, but they said you might be in the locker room... And all the upperclassmen seem to know my name."

"Oh... really. So, why were you looking for me?"

"...If you don't mind, I'd rather talk somewhere else. Do you have time right now?" She looked up at Wataru with eyes so black they looked like they might swallow him.

First Kawamura drew back even more than Wataru at this unexpected request, but Miho didn't look his way. Because she hardly blinked, her unflinching gaze seemed to glimmer coquettishly. Most guys would probably have reeled from being looked at with those eyes, but Wataru just looked back at her in wonder.

She had a surprisingly small face, and her skin was so smooth it reminded him of raw cake batter. Her naturally arched brows were groomed, and she seemed to wearing hardly any makeup. Only her full lips were colored a modest pink, and her hair and her eyes were jet black, in contrast with her pale, fragile-looking limbs that stuck out of her uniform. Maybe that was why he felt like he wanted to protect her, despite the lively impression she made. In short, she was the ideal girlfriend of any guy's dreams.

"He's right... That must be what he meant by the female Kazuki..."

"Fujii?"

"Huh? Oh, right. By somewhere else, do you mean, not at school?"

Instead of nodding, she cracked a smile and kept silent. Maybe since he had such a talkative sister, this kind of reaction was refreshing to him. He wasn't worried at all about what she might ask of him. Wataru took his bag from a stunned Kawamura and led Miho away from the boys' locker room.

"Oh, yeah. Kawamura, thanks a lot for today."

"Huh?"

"I'll call you tonight. Sorry! Gotta go now."

"B-But..." Being robbed of his best friend by the sudden appearance of a beautiful girl—but really wishing *he* had been stolen—Kawamura felt conflicted as he raised his right hand. Even after Wataru and Miho disappeared from the locker

room, he forgot to lower it.

Miho had said that she preferred somewhere out of the way, so after Wataru thought about it, he decided to bring her to the coffee shop where he met Yuichi. He knew they wouldn't have to worry about seeing any other students from their school. For a moment, he did think, *Kazuki wouldn't like this,* but since it was a girl, probably with a delicate problem, and there was no other agenda, he decided that it was the best place.

"Fujii. Um, what do you...think of me?" Without taking a sip of the iced tea that she had ordered, Miho suddenly dove in. Without any prior indication, Wataru couldn't hide his surprise at her directness.

"What do I... I'm not sure I understand..."

"Please tell me honestly. Are you not interested at all? Don't you like me?"

"No, uh... You're pretty... I guess," he stammered, and Miho's serious expression softened a little. She was probably used to being told she was pretty, but if this was an act, she managed an innocent reaction.

She took the ceramic sugar syrup container in her hand, seeming relieved, and turned to Wataru to ask, "How pretty?" Looking at them from outside, they appeared to be the perfect couple.

But unfortunately, Wataru had a boyfriend who he was crazy about. If Miho's business had something to do with love, then to stay a while would probably only invite confusion. As Wataru thought to himself, *I'll head her off early,* as if she had read his mind, she said to him, "You must have things to do. I'll be quick."

She went on, "I knew who you were from before. Like, from the time when everyone was talking about how you and Kazuki had paired rings, right? Or that Kazuki was going out with your sister, or whatever was between the two of you—

there's been all kinds of rumors. So...I knew right away."

"You knew... What?"

"Whose ring it was. A simple silver ring with a thin gold line in the center."

"What?!" His heart started to pound and Wataru involuntarily leaned over the table. "Is it possible? Do you have my ring...?"

"Yes. I found it, in the hallway outside the locker room. I had been lying down in the nurse's office because of my anemia, and I was feeling better so I was on my way back to class. But since there are lots of rings that look like that, I thought I'd better check with the owner... So, after school I went to your classroom."

"But...aren't you a first-year? What were you doing on the second-year floor?"

"I was taking the long way back. It's a good way to waste time, you know?" Miho replied innocently without hesitation, lightly shrugging her delicate shoulders. It was an angelic, mischievous gesture that he had often seen celebrities do on television. Maybe the reason it didn't annoy him was because he had rarely seen it in real life.

Now that they were going along at her pace, he had completely missed the chance to call her into question. "A-Anyway, thanks for finding my ring."

"You're welcome. I'm glad I could help you, Fujii. I thought you were pretty lucky that I found it."

"Why?"

"C'mon, don't pretend with me. Didn't I come on to you before? Didn't you say I was pretty?" Her long eyelashes trembled gracefully, casting a subtle shadow on her skin. With that, the image of a lively girl was gone, replaced by something vague and mysterious. It would have been quite a performance if she was deliberately using all of this to her advantage, in contrast with Yuichi, who was more or less indifferent to his own good looks. Perhaps this was just the difference between guys and girls.

However charming a person was, he couldn't help but compare them with Yuichi, maybe because his heart was already taken by him. But Miho seemed to pick up on that. Suddenly her smile fell, and before Wataru could answer she said, "What's wrong with me?" and sighed. "I'm disappointed. Since I found your ring, I was sure there was some sort of connection between us…"

"Um, where *is* my ring, by the way? I've been looking for it all day."

"I told you, I have it. But this is awful. Have you been listening to what I'm saying?" Displeased, Miho lightly patted the bag at her side with her palm. "Fine. If that's your attitude, maybe I just won't give your ring back."

"Y-You won't give it back? Hey, stop kidding around. I told you it was mine, didn't I?"

"You and Kazuki have both been wearing them on your left ring fingers. So then, if someone finds out that you lost it, they'd be upset, wouldn't they? That's why you were looking around so frantically."

If you know that much, then why don't you just give it back?! The words flew into his throat but Wataru barely managed to swallow them. She was younger, and if he responded aggressively she was likely to get even more cross. He had been schooled in that tactic by his little sister, Karin. But since Miho had not yet specified what it was that she wanted, it probably wouldn't help to keep talking.

"Well… What do I have to do to get back my ring?" It bothered him how poorly that came out, but necessity knows no law. "I'll do whatever I can to accommodate your wishes but…"

"Then, will you go out with me?"

"Huh? Go out?! You and me?!" For a moment, Wataru couldn't believe his own ears. *How the hell had this become the solution?!* But he was more astonished that Miho, who had just mentioned that there was someone else who would be upset, now sat with a sense of entitlement, primly smiling with her nose turned up.

"Fujii, you want your ring back, don't you? So why don't you go out with me as a conditional exchange? Then I'll give it back to you. What do you say?"

She drove a hard bargain with that sweet voice. If he just listened to its sound, he would probably think he was simply hearing a pretty, selfish girl. But Wataru shook his head, pale-faced. He couldn't comprehend how she could ask him to go out with her, as if nothing had happened, despite knowing that he had a partner. There were things that he would and wouldn't do for the ring. "Sorry, but I'm in love with someone else. So I can't go out with you."

"But don't you need the ring?"

"I don't think you'd like it if that was the reason I'd go out with you."

"You don't know without trying." Miho idly stirred her straw, pouting her soft lips.

A long silence went on, and Wataru sank down, not knowing what to do. He had plenty of experience with girls asking him out, but Miho wasn't like any of them. First of all, she wasn't behaving as he would expect towards a guy she really liked. Even though she was pretty, she was acting like a princess, with a touch of defiance, too. Normally, when someone confessed their feelings, they had a more modest expression, but she seemed like she was about to pressure him.

Wait, she had *pressured him*...he hurried to correct himself. If she would give the ring back if he said yes, that meant she wouldn't give it back if he refused. He was sure that Miho was fully aware of how irreplaceable the ring she had found was to Wataru. That meant she had a brilliant threat on her hands.

But if Kazuki were to find out that I had lost the ring...that would suck. His Kazuki, who was studying his heart out in order to win the bet with Wataru. But the essential thing was that Wataru had lost his precious ring. And now this girl was using that against him. If Yuichi knew that, he had no idea what he would do, but he was pretty sure that he would hate him for it. And even if Yuichi wasn't shocked and angry, no doubt he would be extremely disappointed. Wataru knew he didn't want to see that fallen expression on Yuichi's face, and needless to say he didn't want to be the cause of it.

"So, Fujii. Why wouldn't you do it? Don't you want your ring back?" Miho seemed irritated, like something was bothering her. Wataru tried to think. Wasn't there a way to get his ring back from her? But before he could come up with anything, she spurred him on. "Say something!"

He had no choice. He gave up and decided to play fair. "There's no way that I can go out with you…"

"'No way'?"

"But if there's something else that you want me to do, I'll do whatever. I promise. So…"

"Something I want you to do? Hmm…" Drumming her cherry-colored nails on her glass, Miho made a face like she could have been humming to herself. For a short time, she looked like she was pondering this. Wataru was rather impressed. Yuichi didn't express his feelings much and often, before Wataru knew it or even knew why, he was in a bad mood. In this way, Miho would be a good girlfriend. "So then, why don't we start out being friends?"

"No matter where we start, all we can ever be is friends."

"Fine, then why don't we do that? Once you get to know me, you might even start to like me. So let's first be friends, okay?"

"…Okay. We'll be friends. So, the ring…"

"I'll hold on to the ring for a little while. Otherwise, you might default on your promise."

"H-How can you…?!" At that outburst, Wataru shut his mouth. Now he didn't understand the point of the conditional exchange.

Miho smiled as she looked at the completely pale Wataru. There was no doubt that he mood had improved as his expression had worsened. She parted her lips like a little devil and warned him in a mature voice, "Now Fujii, I didn't say I would never give it back. The point is, it's a good thing to be nice to me. The quicker we become friends, the faster you'll get your ring back. All you need is a little patience. So don't be cold to me. Got it?"

"When you say quickly become friends…until when…"

"Until I say so." She was definitely enjoying the situation.

As he became aware of this, Wataru fell into hopeless despair. He thought about yelling at her and trying to steal back his ring, but if he dared such a rash move and she hadn't brought the ring here, then she would never give it back to him. He was flooded with feelings—the ring was more precious than the most expensive jewels, and he didn't want to lose it.

But… why, of all people, did a girl like this have to be the one to find it…?

First the exam bet, and now with the ring, he could only feel like he had been cursed. Wataru sighed deeply, and as he sunk into gloomy thoughts, he stared back at the sweet, smiling face before him.

Just as Wataru was dragging his exhausted body into his room, he heard the sound of his cell phone ringing. That would be Kawamura calling, as promised. He hurriedly pulled his phone out of his bag and quickly started to complain about the Miho incident.

"Hey, listen to this, Kawamura…"

"This is Kazuki."

"Huh?!" Wataru turned pale as he heard the voice on the other end and he checked the display dial. It unmistakably showed both the first and last name, Yuichi Kazuki. But he must have been calling from his house phone. If it had been his cell, Wataru had set a special ring tone (he changed it periodically—currently it was "Wish Upon a Star") so that he would know it was him. Caught up in the sudden awkwardness, he couldn't respond.

"Hello? Hey, are you there?"

"Yeah…I'm listening. Sorry, I was confused. Kazuki, are you using your home phone?"

"Yeah, my cell's charging. But there's something I want to ask you about."

What could it be? Wataru thought as he put a hand to his chest where a cloud had started to form. There had to be a reason why he had rushed to call without even waiting for his phone to charge. But Wataru feared that it wasn't a good one. It could have been that he was still feeling guilty about the deal he had made with Miho.

"What is it? It's been a long time since you called me, hasn't it?" Trying his best to seem casual, Wataru's words sounded strained. "You've been studying hard, haven't you? Everyone at school's talking about it."

"Wataru, did you lose your ring?"

"Huh…" As Yuichi cut directly to the point, Wataru turned completely white. Stunned, he heard Yuichi pause to sigh. He was probably on the other end, furrowing his finely-shaped brow, no doubt the shade of his eye color deepening. Wataru struggled to regain himself. He was seized by a strong urge not to lie to him for any reason. But whatever happened, he couldn't let anything upset Yuichi. That was the best way for him to express his love, he thought.

"Wh-What do you mean?" Taking a deep breath so as not to spill his story, Wataru said in a jocular tone, "What's wrong, Kazuki? I'm surprised you'd ask something so strange all of a sudden."

"Just as I was leaving school, I heard something about you losing your ring, that there was a big fuss in the locker room.

I was concerned so I went to your classroom, but you had already gone."

"Oh... really? So I missed the chance for us to go home together?"

"So, what happened? Is it true that you lost your ring?"

"That's a false rumor." Even he was surprised by how easily the words came out. The strange thing was that, as he spoke them, they seemed to become true. He quickly relaxed and continued to speak calmly to Yuichi. "You and I both know how random gossip can be, right? I did take my ring off for gym class, but I guess that's how strange misunderstandings happen."

"So then, you have it...?"

"Of course." Wataru clearly heard the relief in Yuichi's voice, and his heart keenly ached. He had a strong desire to see him right away. If he could just see his face, he would reassure him over and over that everything was all right. "I'm sorry, Kazuki... for causing you to worry."

"No, *I'm* sorry. But it only makes it harder that we haven't spent much time together. I felt so nervous when I heard that you had lost your ring. But as long as it was just a rumor."

"That's right... We haven't been alone together since this term started."

"Wanna do something tomorrow?"

"Yeah..."

"Just hearing your voice makes me miss you, Wataru. Why don't we meet, even if it's just for a little while. After school, at that coffee shop. Do you have time for some iced tea?"

"Uh...sure!" Accepting the sudden invitation, a loud bell went off in Wataru's head. The dark feelings of just a moment ago were dispersed in a flash. Suddenly his view seemed brighter.

They confirmed the time the next day, and then they both hung up on a completely different note from the start. But Wataru was then seized with self-disgust. He had lost the chance to confess the whole ring incident. Now that he had lied about it, all he could do was get the ring back from Miho. And quickly, at that. Otherwise, it would be terrible if he didn't have it by the time Yuichi get his test results.

"Just friends... What is that girl thinking?!"

For now, his problem was tomorrow's date. What excuse could he make to Yuichi about his ring not being on his finger? With the onset of this new puzzle, it looked like he wouldn't be getting much sleep tonight.

"Why... Why are you here?!"

Inside the coffee shop, Wataru headed towards Miho with an expression of disbelief. "Y-You and I don't have any plans?! Not today..."

"I know. You have plans with someone else, right? It's okay, don't pay any attention to me. I just came here to have some iced tea," Miho answered innocently, looking happily at the chilled glass in front of her. Even though it was mid-September, the past several days had continued to be rather warm, so that seemed like a reasonable excuse. But by the look of her mischievous expression, it was clear that she had been waiting here. All the more so because just as Wataru had walked in, in high spirits, she had waved to him with her right hand as if she had been expecting him.

Luckily, Yuichi did not seem to be here yet. Somehow he would convince her to leave before he arrived. He hurried to sit down in the chair she offered across from her. "...How did you know that I would be here today?"

"When I went to your classroom, I talked to the same guy you were with yesterday. He told me you had said over and over how happy you were that you had a date."

"But then, why did you...?"

"I thought maybe this might be where you'd meet. I mean, it was just a hunch. Don't you think I'm pretty quick? Couldn't I be a detective?"

He had no idea how he was supposed to reply to being questioned so nonchalantly.   Without noticing Wataru's stunned expression, Miho started talking again.

"Let's see how sharp I am about something else. The person who will be here soon is Kazuki, isn't it?"

"Huh?!"

"Aw, Fujii, you're so cute! You seem awfully fidgety, I get that this is a special friend. But I wouldn't think that, normally, you would use such an out-of-the-way place to meet someone who was just a friend… Bingo, right? That's why you said you couldn't go out with me, right?"

He didn't know how much of the truth she knew (or thought she knew), but there was a note of certainty in her voice. Yet there was no way Wataru could reply. He couldn't cause Yuichi any more trouble with his own careless actions, and Miho's persistent intentions were still a mystery to him. But if he hesitated much longer, she and Yuichi would end up crossing paths. Backed into a corner, as a last resort Wataru decided to wait for Yuichi outside the café.

But then.

"You…"

"Hello, Kazuki. You're ten minutes late."

Rarely ever encountering anyone in their school uniform here, Yuichi stopped as he entered the café. Wataru hurriedly stood up, embarrassed at having been caught sitting at the same table with Miho. "Uh, um… She's…"

"Miho Ookusa. Nice to meet you. I was pestering Fujii to introduce me to you. Since you're so popular at our school, now I can brag to my friends."

While Miho was smoothly introducing herself, Yuichi's expression didn't even register surprise. Wataru could easily tell from the chill air that Yuichi was cross. Miho didn't seem to mind at all but Wataru wanted to run away it was so uncomfortable.

Of course Yuichi was put-out. Of all people, to have a girl literally come between them at their meeting place that no one else was supposed to know about.

Meanwhile, Miho was taking advantage of Wataru not having a good excuse and she kept right on talking. She seemed completely unaware of Yuichi's cold gaze. On the contrary, the worse the atmosphere got, the livelier she became. Even Yuichi, who had first seemed annoyed, was oddly aware of this.

"Oh, you're looking at me with such a strange expression. Fujii brought me to this place yesterday, so I begged him to come along."

"Yesterday? Wataru brought you here?"

"Yes, that's right. I didn't know about this hideaway. And their iced tea is delicious."

That's what did it for Yuichi. He was beyond sullen, his face became expressionless. He glanced at Wataru with eyes that had lost all traces of warmth and, without saying a word, reversed his steps.

"Kazuki…!"

At this turn of unforeseen circumstances, Wataru regained himself. He tried to rush out after Yuichi, but that glance over his shoulder stopped him in his tracks. Even if he ran up to him now, he was sure to be rejected. What clinched it for him was that icy look. Still unwilling to give up, Wataru called after him desperately. His voice trembled ridiculously, and this was what shifted Yuichi's expression slightly. It wasn't that he was angry; he was just extremely confused. The mere effort to understand why Wataru would bring a girl to their meeting place was enough to depress him. Not wanting to show his true feelings, he needed to get out of there as fast as possible.

"Kazuki…"

"Sorry, Wataru. There's something I forgot I have to do. Another time, okay?" As the monotone words spilled from his lips, Yuichi left the café by himself.

"Don't look at me with such a scary face. We're friends, aren't we?"

"We may be friends, but cutting in like that? Come on, give me back the ring..." Wataru wearily sat back down in the chair, literally holding his head in his hands. On his left ring finger, in place of his ring, he had wrapped a big bandage. After thinking about it all night, this was the makeshift excuse he had come up with to explain why he wasn't wearing his ring, but Yuichi had left before he even had a chance to make it.

"Maybe you should wear a ring that looks just like it, for camouflage," Miho murmured casually as she cast a glance at Wataru's bandage. "You can't keep saying that you hurt yourself. Kazuki, nor anyone else, would be able to tell from far away. You shouldn't worry about it."

"......"

"Really, it isn't just coincidence that your rings match, is it? It's on-purpose, and you're both wearing them on your left ring fingers, right? Then, when Kazuki saw me, he took off. So that means the rumor about you two going out must be true."

She made her assertion in a voice full of confidence, staring with pleasure at Wataru, who wasn't saying anything. The glimmer in her pretty black eyes, like a small bird's, seemed to deepen dramatically. This was a very charming effect but Wataru, unfazed, once again dropped his gaze to the table. Just as if she were a girl sitting before her boyfriend, Miho's eyes changed back to the color of love. All this happened in the short time it took to bring Wataru a glass of water. When he once again raised his head, she again had on the face of a prim little devil.

"Hey, why aren't you saying anything? Admit it, or explain it to me!"

"No matter what I say, I'll only make it worse for Kazuki.

Everybody knows him in our neighborhood. You probably don't realize this, but even careless remarks have an effect on Kazuki. I've already caused him trouble in the past, I don't want to make the same mistake again."

"You mean the rumor about your little sister? Kazuki really came after you, didn't he?"

"How do you know about that?" Feebly, Wataru let out a bitter smile, turning his thoughts to the departed Yuichi. How wretchedly would he think of Wataru, now that he had brought a girl and not even made any excuses, after Yuichi had made time in his busy schedule to meet him? Seized by the powerless feelings of not having his ring on his hand, he couldn't summon his usual resolve. On the contrary, even his confidence in Yuichi's love for him seemed like nothing but a daydream. Wataru had to remind himself that their rings had become a means of support when they couldn't be together all the time.

But now there was Miho. More than the fact that she had his ring, allowing her to infiltrate Kazuki was risky. He didn't know what her real intentions were, but he couldn't just ignore them.

Whether or not she knew what he was thinking, Miho finished off the last of her iced tea and got up first from her seat. "Fujii, I'm not who you think I am."

"Huh?"

"I can be pretty cheeky, but really I didn't mean anything by it."

"What do you mean?"

"Just what I said. The one who got injured was Kazuki, but you're the one who seems to be in pain. It's like you're out-of-whack. When I saw how upset you looked, I thought I'd give you back the ring but…instead now I don't want to anymore."

"B-But, c'mon…!"

The last part was almost as if he was talking to himself.

Wataru couldn't believe how rude she was being, but Miho didn't seem to care in the least. From her wallet she took out what she owed for the check and lightly put it down in front of Wataru. "Since we're friends, we can go dutch," she tossed out defiantly. The smiling face she left him with was undoubtedly princess-like; however, somehow it seemed slightly more immature than usual.

From then-on, regardless of what other people thought, Miho attached herself to Wataru. At first, the other students watched with curiosity, but since her attitude was so open, they quickly got used to it. The one who was truly unhappy was Wataru. Just like with Yuichi, now he became the object of envy and jealousy of the male students, and he was definitely sick of it. Wataru was only able to tolerate it because he had Kawamura, who understood the situation and would listen to his complaints.

"But, what could Miho be thinking?" Kawamura said, with warm, fried noodle bread from the cafeteria in one hand. "Today, it will have been one week. Everyone's saying that you guys are going out. What if it gets out to Yuichi? You know he'll be mad."

"But it's not like I can go around saying, 'Yuichi Kazuki is the man I love.' That would be an even bigger mess, wouldn't it? And since he ran out of the coffee shop... he's been so cold. I know it was all my fault, but still..."

Wataru lost his appetite, and with a sigh, he pushed his own bread towards Kawamura. In truth, that night he had sent Yuichi an email apology right away but there had been no response, and since the following day he hadn't seen him at all, even at school.

"But, you know, I hear he's studying like crazy. He never leaves the classroom; I haven't seen his face even once. C'mon, do you think he's mad at me?"

"Well...he's probably just busy. There's only one week left

before the exams…"

The real reason why Kazuki was studying like crazy for his exams was that winning the bet with Wataru depended on the results. Despite that fact, since things weren't going well between the two of them, it only seemed more and more pointless. Even if Yuichi did rank in the top thirty, would they really be able to fulfill the original goal? Moreover, Miho stubbornly refused to give back his ring.

"Your problems keep piling up. Man, the path of love is thorny."

"Kawamura… You think this is funny?"

Throwing an innocent look in Wataru's direction, Kawamura kept eating his fried noodle bread in silence. Right now, Yuichi must be having lunch too, Wataru thought, as he suddenly had the urge to go see him in his classroom. Yet, even when things were normal he restrained himself, and now with things being up in the air like they were, it would probably only attract more attention. This was the burden he bore for having the stud of the century as his boyfriend.

Giving up, he stared at Kawamura while he ate. Suddenly, Kawamura's eyes fell upon Wataru's ring finger.

"Hey, you got your ring back, did you?"

"Oh, this isn't it. It looks just like it, but it's a fake. I had to, I couldn't keep lying with the bandage, and I didn't want Kazuki to hear that I wasn't wearing my ring. So yesterday I bought one that could pass for it from far away."

"Wow…you found a pretty good one. Well, that might have something to do with a new rumor then."

"A new rumor…?" Wataru couldn't let Kawamura's words go by, and he knit his brows together earnestly. In truth, he had had enough of the rumors, but once he heard them, he couldn't just ignore them. "Are they saying something else about me? Besides the stuff about Miho?"

"Uh, well… Listen, you know they say you guys are going out, right? This is related, I guess the rumor is that you and she were in a store buying a ring, I heard something like that this morning. But now I get it. Miho must have been with you when you went to buy it."

That was exactly what had happened, and Wataru, annoyed now, nodded vigorously. She had been the one to suggest that he use a decoy in the first place, and she had found one that had almost the same design as the original. So he had involuntarily ended up taking her to the store with him. At first he had insisted that he was going on his own, but then she threatened not to tell him where it was, so he had no choice, and that was how they ended up going together.

"...Wow, and that was just yesterday? I've got to be more careful about who sees me where. Good grief!"

"Well, that's just proof that you're popular now. I've never had... not once..."

"What's the matter, Kawamura?"

All of a sudden, his friend's words broke off, and Wataru's gaze narrowed in curiosity. But Kawamura's eyes flew from Wataru and riveted on someone else above him. Before Wataru could turn around, he felt the person closer. While he wanted to follow the movement of his gaze, Wataru felt a shadow fall over the top of his head.

"Sorry to bother you while you're eating."

"Ka-..."

"There's something I want to talk to you about. Can you come with me?"

"Kazuki..."

Even though it was Wataru he was speaking to, Kawamura also nodded his head nervously. Wary of people's attention, the two of them hardly ever had daily exchanges at school. That said, the fact that Yuichi was here now was probably due to some sort of problem. It could have been that he was tired from studying, but the glint in his eyes was especially sharp, and there was something sinister in his expression, which was full of intensity. Wataru shyly raised himself out of his seat and sent an anxious glance towards Kawamura.

"Don't look at me like that. I didn't come here to torment you."

"Uh…I know…" Why was it that the more he tried to deny it, the more anxious he became? Steeling himself, Wataru took a short, deep breath and, attracting the attention of his classmates, he followed Yuichi out of the classroom.

"C'mon, Kazuki. Where are we going?"

"How many hideaways do you think I have in this school? The student council office, of course!" Dangling the same key as he looked back, Yuichi answered brusquely. When he had been angry about the Karin rumor and had dragged Wataru off, it had also been to the student council office. That time, in the middle of their argument, he had suddenly kissed Wataru, though it had ended with Wataru slapping Yuichi and declaring that they were through. Seized by a strange sense of *déjà vu*, Wataru unconsciously said a little prayer to himself. *Please don't let it end so awkwardly this time!*

Entering the room and locking the door from inside, first Yuichi sank deeply into one of the tubular chairs. He touched his chin, and as Wataru saw the ring on his left ring finger glimmer he felt a sense of relief.

"It seems like whenever I bring you here, I'm always angry."

"Oh… So you *are* angry with me…"

"You don't sound surprised, so you must have an idea why."

The relief was only momentary. Now, Yuichi stared intently at Wataru, who was standing before him. Normally, his competitive spirit wouldn't allow him *not* to say something in response, but all that he wanted to do was surrender completely and have everything back to normal.

But! He almost let out a sigh involuntarily. How could he explain so that Yuichi would be convinced? To tell him about

Miho, the ring incident was essential, and then he would have to let him know that he had lost it and she had found it. And Wataru had already lied to him about that. He didn't think that he would be easily forgiven for such an offense.

While Wataru was worrying about all this, it seemed like finally Yuichi could no longer stand the silence. Freely, since no one was watching, with the sour face that he never showed to anyone else, he said, "...I know it's my decision to take the exams, and that I was the one who decided to try to rank in the top thirty. So what I'm about to say is probably ridiculous..."

"......"

"But, when I'm studying like crazy, and I think of you having fun with that girl, I get mad."

"I-I'm not having any fun. The girl, she's just a friend, that's all."

"Really? Well, the whole school is saying that you guys are going out. I don't care about that false rumor. I'm the one you're really going out with, but you can't have it both ways."

Yuichi ran his left hand through his bangs, which cast his handsome face in shadow. Seeing this, Wataru wondered when was the last time he had seen Yuichi smile. Recently, because of all the troubles they'd had, the only impression he had was of him sighing depressively. That made Wataru very sad, and he hung his head limply.

Seeing his boyfriend in such a silent state, Yuichi let out another deep sigh. "Do you think I haven't heard all this worthless gossip? Before, it was that you had lost your ring, and now... I heard that you gave a ring as a present to that first-year girl. When I heard that, I snapped, and as soon as I could, I headed for your classroom. Whether or not it's a false rumor, all this talk about your ring pisses me off. That's the one thing...I can't just smile and pay no attention to it."

"I-It's a complete lie! That's... It's because..."

"Because what?"

"Because it's…it's all just crap…"

He couldn't explain the fact that he had bought a ring, there was too much back-story. *But it's true that I bought a ring, although I can't explain exactly why, because…*

Thinking this, he could only manage to deny it with a feeble voice, which only encouraged Yuichi's misgivings. He grilled him with what seemed like irritation.

"All right, Wataru. If it's really not true, then look me in the eye and deny it. Why would those rumors keep coming up—if you know why, please tell me. If not, then…"

"What?"

"I don't what I'll do…to that first-year."

"You don't know what you'll *do*?!"

Wataru found it difficult to tell for sure whether Yuichi was making a threat or just kidding around. He had changed a little, but usually Yuichi was the ideal boyfriend with regard to other girls, always acting like a gentleman. That was why his ring had sent such ripples through the girl students. Now all of a sudden it was hard to believe it was Yuichi who uttered the dangerous words, "I don't what I'll do."

The way he firmly pursed his lips emphasized his determination. When Wataru realized this was really how Yuichi felt, he became extremely sad. He had caused the Yuichi he dearly loved to utter such out-of-character words. And it was all because he had carelessly lost his own ring. Then he had been afraid of falling out of his favor, and he had continued to lie.

"Kazuki, I'm sorry…" Before he realized it, the words were out of his mouth. "I know you're angry about what's been happening. That must be why you didn't reply to my email, right?"

"…No that's not why. I was just thinking about things. Like the things that I said… Why am I forcing myself to study so hard that I don't see you? That time in the coffee shop, when I met her, I got pretty depressed. It seemed like what I'm doing is so pointless, so I don't really know what to say to you."

"Really… Do you really think there's no point?!" Wataru was a little taken aback, and without realizing it he raised his voice. Yuichi opened his eyes wide at his sudden change from solemn to upset. It seemed like only now, at this fresh expression of Wataru's voice, that the color in his eyes returned.

"If that's how you feel, then what's the point of me supporting you? That's not how I wanted it in the first place. Not only was it painful not to be able to see you, wasn't the object of that bet whether we'd go to bed or not…?"

"Wataru…"

"When I saw how hard you were studying, the two seemed so unrelated. That's when I made up my mind, that no matter what the results are, you and I… We'll…"

This essential point formed in his mind before it could even become words. Struggling with his own impatience, he was overcome with ardor and he pleaded with Yuichi.

"Didn't I tell you last time that I will always love you? I know that the thing with Miho is unpleasant…I sincerely apologize with all of my heart. But there's absolutely no reason for you to worry. I think the fact that you're working so hard is cool. It's not pointless at all."

"……"

"Whatever ranking you are in the exams, I want to go to bed with you."

When he made that confession, Yuichi abruptly reached out his left hand. His long fingertips softly brushed Wataru's lips. His neatly trimmed nails slowly traced their outline, and the clean scent of soap tickled Wataru's nostrils. Trying to still his racing heart, Wataru turned towards Yuichi with a searching look. When he parted his lips slightly and softly bit down on his fingertips, he looked back at him with loving smile.

"The only reason I'm studying so hard is to sleep with you."

The soft murmur of his voice quietly echoed in the room. Yuichi slowly got up from his chair and put his arms around Wataru.

"Do you think that my motive is cool?"

"All the more so. Kazuki, you're my...boyfriend, after all."

"Then don't get so familiar with other people that you start rumors. I'll forgive you for breaking the rules by bringing someone to our café, but you'd better think long and hard about it."

"I know, I'm sorry. I won't do it again."

From the bottom of his heart, Wataru nodded, accepting the shower of criticism. Yuichi's true feelings were revealed by what he said. He could do away with all the indirect words, and after just holding each other things would be fine. Feeling his body heat through his back was all he needed to dispel his senseless anxiety.

"Sorry... Kazuki..."

"It's all right. I should be more understanding. Even though all I'm doing is complaining to you about being angry about the gossip, really I just ached to hold you. Every day, I can't get enough of you. I realize that now that we're alone together."

Yuichi sighed and added, "I surrender. I missed you." Wataru slowly looked up at him from within his arms and saw that he wore a weak smile. Even Yuichi was surprised by how he gave in to Wataru and he sighed to himself. But it was a sigh full of satisfaction and content.

"I missed you so much, too. When I don't see your face, I start to lose the ability to smile myself. See, now I'm really smiling, aren't I?"

"Yes, you are. The first time I saw you, you were smiling just like that." As Yuichi spoke, he pulled Wataru even tighter in his embrace. Then he whispered in his ear the same words as when he had first confided his love, "I've never seen a smile like that before."

"Kazuki…"

"It was at that moment that I fell in love with you."

"……"

Almost dizzy with happiness, Wataru closed his eyes to drink in the moment. Before long, he felt a hand on his chin, and as his face was gently turned upwards the pleasing sensation continued.

"Wataru…"

As the soft lips closed on his, a numbness spread out from the place where their mouths met. After taking several short breaths, Yuichi started kissing him deeply all over again. At the same time his arms tightened around his back, and he embraced him so tightly he could barely breathe. Although his kiss was quite passionate, there was still something dutifully gentlemanly about it. When he kissed him this way, Wataru thought his whole heart would melt. Even now, the strength left his body, and it was almost as if he was entrusting Yuichi to keep him standing.

"Wataru, I love you…"

As if to caress the increasing warmth, little by little Yuichi's kisses moved along his skin from his lips to the nape of his neck. As he breathed into his hair and neck, Wataru couldn't stop his body from trembling violently.

"K-Kazuki…?" Sensing that something was slightly different, he tried to call out his name. But unfortunately the passionately enflamed Yuichi didn't seem to hear him. Yuichi gently nipped at the place where his lips were, and Wataru made a short intake of breath. Behind his eyes, he felt a glimmer, and there was no way he could let this pleasure pass him by. It was not uncomfortable at all, but since it was the first time he had let anyone touch him there, he didn't know how to respond and was confused. Soon Yuichi began to suck harder around his ear and his nape, and against his will he couldn't help but cling to Yuichi's body. When he felt the tip

of his wet tongue move towards his collarbone, knowing that he was helpless, he still couldn't manage to shove him away.

"K-Kazuki, stop... C'mon, wait...!"

When it seemed like these few words would not stop him, Wataru blocked his lips. His fiery hot fingertips fluttered over his warm skin, and Wataru turned red again at the new sensation that his lips experienced.

At some point, the top buttons on Wataru's uniform shirt had come undone, and Yuichi could see part of his bare chest. As he made a move to bring his lips there, Wataru finally couldn't stand it anymore. Thrusting out both of his arms and struggling to escape, Yuichi still wouldn't let him go, and Wataru got angrier and angrier. If he were pushing him over, little by little, towards the floor, then all their waiting and arguing until now would indeed have been pointless. Simply to give up his body to his impulses in the heat of the moment, it was too much for the sacrifices he had already made.

As Wataru regained his sense of reason, he said spitefully at the top of his voice, "Kazuki! The exam results aren't out yet!"

"Uh..." His eyes were engorged with passion, but with that single utterance Yuichi stopped everything that he was doing. Then he blinked several times, his expression gradually returned from a dream to reality. After his eyes awkwardly met the now fully disgruntled Wataru's, his voice cracked with a dazed murmur—what else he could say? "...Sorry... I guess... It's just been so long since I felt the warmth of your body, it's like my brakes are loose or something..."

"......"

"I'm really sorry. So don't look at me that way."

It may have been that even Yuichi didn't fully understand his own impulses. As if he were looking at a strange creature, he stared at his two hands, deeply lost in his own thoughts. *It's not your hands, it's your lips that are the problem,* Wataru wanted to say, but since he hadn't rejected his advance from the start, he felt like he was also to blame, so he remained silent.

With his eyes on his fingers, Yuichi let out a murmur as if he was talking to himself. "Really... Top thirty in the whole country, I think that'd be difficult even for me."

"What...?" Slightly taken aback, Wataru hurriedly looked at Yuichi's face. "If that's the case, then why did you...?"

"You know how stubborn I can be. That time, it was the truth when I said that I wanted to sleep with you... But, when you were upset by that fastball I threw you, it was pretty awkward, wasn't it? So I thought I would tack on as high a value as possible. If I hadn't, would you have accepted the proposal and said, 'Okay, after the exams...'? Of course, that *was* pretty charming. But even though I'm stubborn, I wanted us to go to bed together at my own pace, too. Otherwise..." Yuichi broke off there.

Now Yuichi seemed swallowed-up by his boyishness. He had committed an offense and there was nothing he could do. His eyes were all twisted up, and he kept them on the floor with a sulky pose. Shamefully biting his lip, without looking at Wataru at all he said, "I'm the only one who acts like he's in love. I miss you, I want you, I get upset."

"Kazuki...."

"So let's clear this ridiculous condition, I want to put *you* first."

Wataru started to feel like he had when Yuichi confessed his love. He hadn't known what to do just now, when he had shouted at him angrily, but he was grateful that his purely imaginary fears were gone.

Without the slightest awareness that Wataru was moved, Yuichi continued speaking with a grave look on his face. "When I first fell in love with you, I didn't know what to do about having a crush on a guy, so I was at a loss. But then even after it was mutual, there was still a lot of trouble. Of course, they were happy troubles so I didn't mind. That's just how I feel sometimes. When it's a crush, it's like you just love someone irrationally. But maybe it's these restrictions that are actually essential in creating feelings of real love."

"What about restrictions…?"

"Right. Before, it was enough to just secretly carry around the matching ring. But now, even though I know that your heart is mine, the stakes are even higher. Even when we're apart, I feel sad when I think you're not wearing your ring, or I can't forgive you for giving someone else a ring. By higher stakes, I mean it's become restrictive, in a way. Don't you think?"

At last Yuichi returned his gaze and slowly drew closer to Wataru.

"But, if I can be together with you, Wataru, it doesn't matter how restricted I may be…"

"Wh-Why…"

"Restricted happiness is better than the freedom of solitude." Standing in front of Wataru, Yuichi smiled as he took both of his hands lovingly. Absent-mindedly thinking about restricted happiness, Wataru carelessly forgot about his ring and gave his left hand to Yuichi.

And then.

"Wataru… This…" The gentle voice had changed its tune, and Yuichi's eyes quickly darkened in shadow.

"This isn't my ring…is it?"

"Uhhh… Ah!"

As the words came out of Yuichi's mouth, the atmosphere in the room entirely changed. Perhaps he couldn't believe what he saw with his own eyes, and for quite a long time his gaze remained fixed on Wataru's left ring finger. Doubt and confusion, as well as bewilderment…one by one, complicated emotions floated up and then disappeared in Yuichi's eyes.

"Uh, umm… It's not what you think, Kazuki. The whole thing is…"

"It looks just like it, but this one has two thin gold lines."

"……"

"Wataru, my ring… What happened to it?"

He couldn't believe that this low voice came from the same person who had just declared his love. Wataru tried with all his strength to pull back his hand, but Yuichi reflexively refused to let go. He held his wrist even more strongly, and the dull pain contorted Wataru's face. But what pained him even more was his own foolishness at not having any excuse, yet this was nothing compared with the shock that he had given Yuichi.

No matter how he explained, it wouldn't change the fact that the ring was gone. Nevertheless, he had to at least say something. Wataru racked his brain. It would have been fine if Yuichi had stayed fierce, but after he had confided his feelings with such unusual honesty, maybe he just didn't have the strength left. With eyes that conveyed so much fixed upon Wataru, he didn't say another word. The silence weighed down upon Wataru more than any speech.

The end-of-lunch bell rang out in the awkward silence. Yuichi quietly let go of the hand he had been grasping while letting out an exhausted sigh. If only he hadn't lied, he could have said that he left it at home, but since he had on this fake that made it clear that he had made-up a story, he wouldn't even bother to give him a hard time. And if he told him that this was the ring he had bought with Miho, his credibility would be called into question. Yuichi would have no way to know whether to believe Wataru.

"Should we go…?"

He shook his head firmly from side to side at the obligatory words, and Yuichi quietly handed him the room key.

"Well, I'm gonna go first then. You can hold onto the key for a little while."

"So then…you mean I won't see you for a while?"

"…Exams are soon."

Answering him with these few words, he left Wataru and

walked out. Last time at the coffee shop, Yuichi hadn't heard his voice, but Wataru knew now that even if he called out he wouldn't turn around. He didn't even try to hold him back.

Now, more than ever, the least he could do was get his ring back.

Newly-resolved, Wataru could hardly wait until after school to find Miho. Since usually she was the one to invite him to leave school together, this time her irked "friend" had come to ask her, and Miho seemed to be in high spirits. But when she saw that they were going to a family restaurant instead of the coffee shop, instantly she started to voice her discontent. "Hey, I like that place. The old man's iced tea is delicious…"

"Sorry, but you can't go back there. That's what we decided."

"…He gave you a hard time, didn't he? Because I closed-in on your special meeting place." Even after they were led to their seats in the restaurant, Miho still seemed piqued, but since Wataru wasn't budging, eventually she relented.

"Today will be your treat, then," she prefaced, as she ordered the azuki bean parfait and then returned to her normal self.

"Fujii, are you in a bad mood? You've had quite a harsh look on your face this whole time," she asked, smiling innocently as if she had no idea what was going on.

When he asked her, "Whose fault is that?" she immediately replied, "I know why. Kazuki found out about the ring incident, didn't he?"

She went on, "That's what the girls in my class were saying. Kazuki left school early this afternoon. I think he looked so upset, his teacher didn't even ask why he was leaving."

"Really…?"

"You mean, you didn't know? I figured you guys must have had a fight."

"We did. But the situation is much worse than just the fight. I really shocked Kazuki."

"What…"

Despite the calmness of his tone, he spoke the truth. The smile abruptly disappeared from Miho's face. Without looking at the parfait that was brought to her, she stared at Wataru with an earnest look. Whether or not she found this new development interesting, surprisingly she didn't gloat.

"Fujii, you haven't told me what's going on…" Miho said meekly after five minutes of silence. "If you've told me this much already, you might as well just admit it. Kazuki is your boyfriend. Doesn't it make it worse for him if you don't deny or confirm it?"

"Then will you give me my ring back, now that I've done Kazuki wrong?"

"Well…" Miho hesitated for a moment in her reply. Her bold expression crumpled slightly, and the faint glimmer of a normal girl crossed her eyes. But it was only the quickest of moments. She sat up straight and quickly regained herself, defiantly affirming, "Yes…right. Kazuki is a little too good for you. That's why he's mad."

Even though what she said to him was really none of her business, having just seen Miho's brief change, Wataru suddenly became aware of the new fact that had brought it to his attention. Even if he understood, he didn't yet know how to resolve it, since all this time he had only been thinking of the ring and hadn't known what Miho's objective was. But in that moment of quiet expression, she had been thinking deeply of someone. There was probably no point in telling her about "the freedom of solitude."

If that was the case, then the other person must be…

"When I look at you, I think you're pretty crafty," Miho said, batting her jet black eyelashes with an upward glance at Wataru. "You're the one who said that it was no good for Kazuki if everybody made a big fuss, but really you're the one who hates it, aren't you? That's because you guys are a couple. Most people would think that's strange, and then all you'll have is trouble. But the way I see it, only Kazuki will lose his popularity, and that's not such a bad risk to take. It doesn't really matter what people think."

"I-It's all because you won't give me back my ring! That's why I had to have a replacement, but it couldn't have been worse timing for Kazuki to find out..."

"What do you mean? It's your own fault, isn't it? You had to make do with the fake ring because you decided to lie."

"It was your idea, wasn't it? You said I ought to camouflage it." He flashed back defensively because she was using his own argument against him, but he knew full-well that he was reaping what he had sown. When Yuichi had asked him on the phone whether he had lost his ring, if he had promptly apologized then everything would have been fine. Then he wouldn't have fallen into this self-misery.

Miho suddenly picked up her spoon and pointed it right at Wataru's dark face. "Do you like sweets? They make you feel better when you're depressed."

"Miho..."

"Oh, so I've been demoted from 'you,' have I? Soon you'll be calling me Miss Ookusa, huh?" Perhaps she liked hearing Wataru say her name, because a smile escaped her lips. It couldn't compare with any celebrity's fake smile, it was such a pretty and angelic expression. But she soon withdrew it. As if Wataru's heavy feelings were contagious, a dark shadow fell across her eyes. "You and Kazuki, you guys didn't break up, did you?"

"Uh, well..."

"It can't be such a big deal that you lost your ring, can it? Really?"

Miho persisted unusually seriously, but Wataru made no move to reply. Of course, they hadn't actually talked about breaking up, but when he thought about their exchange from lunch, it seemed like it would take a long time to restore Yuichi's lost trust. Even though until now they had always been able to resolve whatever awkward situations by holding each other, this didn't seem that simple. In the first place, he didn't know if Yuichi would even let Wataru touch him again.

"That can't be true. There are all kinds of substitutes for that ring, aren't there? Why is this such a big deal? Everybody else carries around extras, since rings change just like partners do," Miho said, seeming exasperated while eating her parfait with surprising speed.

While he watched her with amazement, Wataru couldn't help but be filled with a quiet sadness in his heart. He hadn't just shocked him, he had probably made Yuichi *hate* him. After losing his beloved ring, he had lied to his face. And with the various conditional exchanges, he had let Miho flirt with him, which caused him unnecessary stress. What would Yuichi even think about someone like that?

"The fake ring...only made things worse..."

Miho's spoon stopped as he mumbled to himself.

"Right... I guess he'll have to ask Toko to make him another one of the real thing."

"What are you muttering to yourself about? Hello?! Are you okay?"

"Miho, sorry, but I'll owe you for today! I've got to go!"

"Huh?! W-Wait a minute! What did you mean, the real thing? Hey, where are you going, Fujii? Wait, I said... Wait!"

Grabbing the check, she rushed after Wataru, who had jumped up from his seat. But Wataru couldn't wait for her. As quickly as he could, he ran off to Toko's store to ask her to make another ring. He would take that to Yuichi's house, and apologize with his whole heart. He didn't know how long he would have to wait on Miho's flighty moods, and in the meantime the huge chasm between Yuichi and him could widen.

Why hadn't he thought of this before, Wataru scolded

himself. Yuichi had asked Toko to make him the ring in the first place. You could say that she was the original creator, which would be totally different from wearing a fake. Even if Miho intended to give back the ring that she held hostage, he could no longer stand for this awkward situation with Yuichi to go on. For that, he needed a true replacement ring.

As Wataru walked on briskly in silence, Miho called out to him over and over. But Wataru made no response. To get to Toko's shop, he would have to change trains several times, and if he didn't hurry the store would be closed. Each day later Yuichi would be further away, and Wataru felt extremely anxious. Whoever it was that Miho loved, none of that made any difference anymore.

"Wow, it's so beautiful. Is this an accessory shop?" Miho squealed with girlish delight as she looked through the window at the jewelry displayed there. She had ended up following him all the way to Toko's store. Unfortunately, Wataru didn't have the mental energy to deal with Miho any more, and he hastily reached for the front door. He felt as if the time when Karin had dragged him here was only yesterday.

I was pretty depressed that time too, wasn't I? Just when he had realized that he was in love with Yuichi, they had parted after a jealous argument over a minor misunderstanding. Since Wataru had never imagined that Yuichi would return his feelings, he had been completely broken-hearted. Compared to his current situation, that now seemed like a rather happy misunderstanding. Just a few hours earlier, in the student council office, when Yuichi had said, "Even after it was mutual, there was still a lot of trouble," Wataru had to agree with him.

"Welcome." As soon as they had stepped into the store, a salesgirl called out in a mild voice from the back of the store. Wataru wished that he could remember whether she was the same woman who had greeted them the first time he came here.

"Excuse me. My name is Fujii, is the owner, Toko…"

"She's in the back… Shall I go and get her?"

"If you don't mind. Would you please tell her I'm here about something very important?" The woman seemed rather bewildered by his forceful reply. Luckily, there weren't any other customers in the shop, since it would probably have disturbed business. Behind him, Miho let out a small giggle, and he glared at her darkly.

While the salesgirl went to get Toko, the store was again engulfed in silence. Casually glancing at his watch, he saw that it was already six o'clock. The store hours posted by the door said they were open until seven, so it seemed he had just made it in time. *I hope this works,* Wataru murmured to himself as Miho, looking in the glass cases, asked, "Are you going to have a ring made?"

She went on, "That must be it. You're going to make a replica of the ring that I found, aren't you?"

"Well, I can't really wait for you to return it to me."

"Oh, so we're back to 'you' now? But it doesn't matter. Why are you so hung-up the ring anyway? You think the love disappears with it?"

"No. That's not it, I just…"

"Just what?"

"I just want to patch things up with Kazuki, that's all…" With no pretenses whatsoever, the words slipped from his lips. Surprised by his own tone, Wataru was speechless. He had been thinking about all the various complications, but it was really that simple. The ring, the bet, the exams, the girl—things had gotten so convoluted, but if Wataru only looked at the basics, he saw that there wasn't any need for further confusion.

"You just want to patch things up with Kazuki…?" Miho repeated, echoing the same surprise as Wataru. As if reciting a spell, her impertinent expression to became that of a defenseless girl. The same way she had been before in the

restaurant, it was as if she herself didn't have any control over the shift. Blushing with dismay when she became aware of Wataru's gaze, she suddenly spouted off. "I... I don't believe this! First a fake and now a replica? Do you think you can just make a fool of Kazuki?! Do you know how lucky you are? To have Yuichi Kazuki all to yourself?! You've got him! And here you are, luring him with a fake ring!"

"Why would you say something like that? You're the one who has…"

"What?! Who do you think had their girlish pride trampled when you said that you wouldn't go out with me?! I was really hurt when you said that. Just look at your face. You haven't lost Kazuki at all, yet there are lots of people who would be fine just to have anyone. But, when a girl asks you to go out with her, how can you just say, 'No way'?!"

"That's… That's not what I said! Even though I was seeing someone, it's not like I could go out with you! In the first place, you…"

"What…?!"

"You weren't after me…"

"Excuse me, you two. Would you mind not making such a commotion in my store?" While they were shouting at each other, Toko took this opportunity to coolly cut in with a commanding tone. Both of them looked up with surprise to see Toko, wearing a pale green pantsuit. "No way!" Miho shouted, not directed towards Toko, of course.

Toko was not alone. Standing a full head taller than Toko, who was wearing three-inch heels, she was accompanied by a young man who stood behind her as if he was her assistant. With his usual haughtiness, his older cousin seemed to raise his head as he stood by her side with a reserved air.

He must have gone home first, because he had changed into a grass-green shirt with three-quarter length sleeves and white cotton pants. His style was enchanting as he stood there not really knowing what to do. Even when he had on a sour look, his neat features seemed to be set, as if a photographer had asked him to pose that way.

"Why…?" *Why are you so damned good-looking…?* Kawamura had called them "stupid couple" but Wataru couldn't help but be infatuated with his looks. No matter when or where, he was the only person in the world who could steal his gaze like that. This was Yuichi Kazuki.

"Kazuki… What are you doing here…?" He mumbled without thinking.

Glancing down at him, still without smiling, Yuichi said, "What do you mean? Toko's my cousin. There's nothing wrong with me coming to visit her."

"You just came to visit? I didn't get the feeling this was some easygoing event."

"Toko." Yuichi glared silently at his cousin who had cut into the conversation.

But as Toko smiled playfully, this time she spoke familiarly to Wataru. "I haven't seen you in a while, Wataru. How is Karin?"

"She's fine, thank you."

"Is this your new girlfriend? I can see by Yuichi and this one, you go for the good-looking ones, don't you, Wataru?"

"Toko!" Yuichi shouted again, unable to control himself.

"Okay, okay, I'm sorry," Toko said, shrugging her shoulders. Then, turning towards a glum looking Yuichi with his arms crossed, "All right, I'll stop playing bad jokes with your heart," she whispered.

"So, Wataru. You told my assistant that you had something important to talk to me about?"

"Oh… I meant…" The conversation suddenly shifted back, but he couldn't ask her anything under these circumstances. Sputtering incoherently, Wataru stared straight back at Toko's smiling face awkwardly.

It had never occurred to Wataru that Yuichi might be here. His vain hopes shattered, he couldn't hide his disappointment, despite his thrill at seeing his boyfriend out of his uniform. He and Miho had been arguing pretty loudly, so he had probably heard the whole thing. Now he knew Wataru had come here to ask Toko to make a replica of the ring. Miho had said, "First a fake and now a replica," and he had a feeling that the punishment would be quickly handed out.

"I'm sorry, Toko. Please forget about what I said," Wataru said, bowing his head deeply as he apologized to her. The timing was so off at this point, the gods were probably telling him that it was useless to even make a replica. Wataru had been obsessively clinging to his ring, but now as he apologized to Toko he felt a little more rational. "It was a stupid idea. But...please don't worry about it."

"I don't understand. Are you sure?"

"Yes. I'm sorry for all this trouble I've caused you." The way things were now, no matter what he did to smooth things over, it would only be awkward. As Wataru raised his head back up, he softly murmured his earlier words to himself, "I just want to patch things up." In his heart, all that he wanted was to be able to enjoy any kind of happiness with Kazuki. To do that, he would stop telling lies, and confess the whole story to Yuichi. It would probably create new ripples, but that was better than the current state of affairs.

"Miho... You were right about what you said earlier."

"What?"

"The person who I'm dating is in fact 'that' Yuichi Kazuki. I have Kazuki all to myself, and he has me all to himself. That's why the ring that you found is more important to me than anything. Yuichi gave it to me, and there are lots of feelings attached to it..."

"Fujii..." Miho listened to Wataru's sudden declaration without blinking. Her eyes seemed the slightest bit damp because they were so large, or perhaps it was due to her own feelings. If this was how it felt to speak so plainly about his relationship with Yuichi, even if he felt self-conscious, he had no regrets.

Feeling eyes upon him, Wataru slowly searched around. His eyes met Yuichi's, who was looking his way while being keenly watched by Toko. His sullen-looking face hadn't changed, but his cold, tense mood had lessened somewhat, and it seemed like he had drawn a little closer. *Will I ever know how Yuichi feels about what I just said?* Wataru thought.

"But Fujii, why are you saying this all of a sudden?" As he turned his attention back to Miho, she frowned as if at something upsetting. "Why? You gave me such a hard time about it being difficultt for Kazuki."

"No, what I meant was that everyone always wants to spread rumors about him. I didn't want to tell you. Even though my best friend and my sister knew the whole story, I figured that eventually it would get out to the school. But like I said before, since Kazuki is always the subject of gossip, his private life is often pried into unnecessarily. So far, there have been lots of unpleasant experiences. That's why I didn't want to give them any more reason to make a fuss. At first…I didn't really understand why you were trying to get close to me."

"……"

"But now I think I do." Even though he had been completely wrapped around Miho's little finger, strangely he didn't dislike her for it. Despite his annoyance at her unrestrained manner with him, he really felt no hatred. It wasn't until today, though, that he realized why.

"While I was watching you eat your parfait today, for some reason I became very sad. You were depressed, but I saw how you tried your best to cheer me up. You thought I was the reason why Kazuki went home early, didn't you? Didn't you think that things had gotten seriously worse between Kazuki and me?"

"But…I never meant to make you two fight…" Miho's huge eyes fell to the floor as she nodded her head. Letting out a sigh of relief, Wataru was surprised when he realized that

Yuichi was coming even closer. It wasn't just a feeling, the distance between them had shrunk, and they looked into each other's eyes silently.

Yuichi's hardened expression had lessened somewhat, and a gentle smile cracked across his eyes and lips. At that moment, his mood brightened, and as he saw this, Wataru too smiled contagiously.

"I only wanted to make trouble for Fujii." Yuichi's eyes tightened a bit at Miho's words. He seemed to be grasping the nature of the relationship between her and Wataru. Unconsciously, he raised his right hand and softly patted Wataru on the back, as if to comfort him.

"I planned to give you back the ring after teasing you a little bit. But then I began to realize…I mean, if I just gave you back the ring, then we wouldn't have become friends, would we?"

"Hey, wait a minute… Do you mean that she has the missing ring that Yuichi came to talk to me about?" Whether or not she meant to, Toko carelessly broke into the conversation. Perhaps this was what gave Miho the courage to timidly raise her head and look back and forth between Yuichi and Wataru standing there.

"Kazuki, don't be angry with Fujii. I stole the ring. While I was coming back from the nurse's office, I saw that the door to the second-year boys' locker room was open, and I just went in there because I was curious. That was when I found it on the floor and I took it."

"Miho… Why would you…"

"I told you, didn't I? I wanted to give you a hard time. I wanted to know what kind of person you were, Fujii. Here was my chance, to use the ring as a pawn. But I never thought you would try so hard to get the ring back. I was confused…"

"You…!"

Yuichi raised his voice and came forward, and Miho quickly stopped talking. But urged on silently by Wataru, who still had a few questions, she reluctantly began speaking again.

"You know, Fujii, even if you hadn't admitted it, I would have known."

"What?"

"That you and Kazuki were actually boyfriends. Because of the gossip it's not as if it was a shot in the dark. That's why I was so jealous of you. It's so embarrassing!" It seemed like even before she had this realization, Miho had seen through them. Instinctively they looked at each other. *What a mess,* Wataru thought as he racked his brain. But he was sure that after the earlier rumors had started, both he and Yuichi had been very careful about what they did.

And still, at school…

"I didn't see anything at school." Shattering their confidence, she patently denied it. "Kazuki, my aunt lives in your neighborhood. You know, the Kanazawa house near the hydrangea grove across from the playground?"

"Oh, the widow's…"

"Is that what you call her? That's a little rude!" Miho sweetly raised her eyebrows and feigned sulkiness. Wataru could tell from that gesture that she had more or less recovered. Indeed, her feminine wiles were less like a blooming flower and more like bold, summer sunshine in their intensity. She was a particularly natural beauty.

"…so, what about Mrs. Kanazawa?" Not amused by the mention of one of his neighbors, Yuichi impatiently prodded her to the point. It seemed like he had completely forgotten about his bygone image as the mild-mannered, ideal boyfriend. "She didn't say anything to you, did she?"

"On the contrary. Around the time when the hydrangeas were in bloom, I happened to see two people kissing in the shadow of the bushes from my aunt's house. I wasn't the only one, my younger sister and my aunt also saw it. 'Don't go telling everybody, now,' my aunt warned me."

"M-Mrs. Kanazawa saw?" Yuichi seemed so shocked, his

voice almost flipped with panic. If that was around the time when the hydrangeas were in bloom, then it was probably when they professed their feelings for each other and had their first kiss. They had only been thinking of themselves, and in their happiness about their mutual love, naturally their lips had come together. That was the scene that she had witnessed.

"But when I see Mrs. Kanzawa in the street, she doesn't act as if…"

"Give her some credit, will you? Why don't you go for a walk with her sometime? She's a fan of yours. She always says, 'If only I were thirty years younger…'"

"Seriously?"

For a moment, Miho looked at Yuichi's flushed face with satisfaction. Then she switched her attention to Wataru, who mumbled in a very faint voice, "I'm sorry."

"I was so jealous of you, Fujii. I mean, ever since I was admitted to this school, I was pining away for Kazuki, before he even knew who I was…I was smitten. If I had been up against another girl, I wouldn't have give up yet, but another boy, of all things. Can you believe it? The upperclassman who all the girls at school are crazy about, secretly dating a younger guy? Can you imagine how I felt when I found out?"

"I'm sorry…" Wataru didn't really know why he was apologizing, but he bowed his head. Even if what Miho said was rather shocking, when he thought about it, this was a natural reaction. Since they had been lucky to have such understanding supporters as Karin and Toko, and even Kawamura, they had been able to go on like this without being bothered. He realized he really couldn't blame Miho. Anybody would be upset about their crush being stolen away by someone of the opposite sex. Wouldn't it make you doubt your own charm? And it was Miho, no less, who was so pretty that guys usually reeled around her.

"All I cared about were my feelings for Kazuki. I never

thought about you…"

"Seriously, how could you say that? I thought it was pretty clear that both of us were in love with Kazuki. Otherwise, why wouldn't I have told everyone? I was shocked, and then depressed. I felt like there wasn't anything I could do."

"R-Really?"

"It's true. And then…you were so cute, too. I mean that as a compliment." Despite what she said, he still had his doubts. As if she were reading those feelings on Wataru's face, Miho laughed strangely, like she couldn't help it. "…Well, here's your ring back."

She reached into the pocket of her summer uniform shirt and raised her finger. Caught on her long, sparkling iridescent nail was his good old silver ring. Miho dropped it into the palm of her left hand and quietly held it out before Wataru. His one and only ring—not a fake or a replica—his precious treasure was finally back in his hand.

"Even when I had it, it was never mine. Not the ring…or you."

"What?" Without comprehending the meaning of her last words, Wataru responded reflexively. But as Yuichi reached his hand out from the side and snatched up the ring, he lost the chance to continue the conversation.

"Ah! What are you doing, Kazuki? Give it back!" Wataru blanched as he pleaded with Yuichi. What would he do if he wouldn't give him the ring back? The Miho incident had been resolved, but there was still the issue of the lies Wataru had told and the unfortunate things he had done.

"Hey, Kazuki! What are you staring at? Give me back the ring."

"It's all right, Wataru. Yuichi's just checking the details for future reference," Toko explained, suppressing a smile. She had been watching their exchange. He sure was checking it thoroughly, holding the ring up to light and fiddling with it, but what did she mean by "for future reference"?

Ignoring Yuichi as he continued to intently examine the ring, Toko took Wataru by the hand and led him into a corner of the store. Then she lowered her voice a bit, and cupped her right hand around her mouth as if she was letting him in on a secret. "I'll tell you why Yuichi came here today."

"Okay…?"

"Actually, it was for the same reason as you. He told me that he wanted me to make another ring like the one from before."

"Huh…" Hearing this totally unexpected news, for a moment Wataru was speechless with amazement. Wataru was the one who had lost the ring, but Yuichi was the one who was more upset about it. When Wataru thought of his reaction, he was so worried that he couldn't make his mouth work for a while.

If Wataru's expression was hard to make out, Toko seemed more and more pleased. "Came to visit me, what a lie," she said, giving him away. She brought her hand back up to her mouth. "He told me that he had lost the ring. But we were worried because we didn't have a mold of it, and thought we'd have to make a new ring. He said he was a little worried that lately you'd been caught up in an issue concerning the ring. But if the feelings haven't changed, then wouldn't a substitute still work?"

"B-But…"

"Of course, it's always better to have the one that your finger's already used to, but to not pay attention to the feelings and only adhere to the vessel would be putting the cart before the horse. I wonder if Yuichi even realized this. If he gave you a new ring, I said, it wouldn't simply be to put his mind at ease. The reason he's looking at the ring so intently is so that, from now on, when something like this happens again, he can ask for an exact replica. It's not just about the design; it's the scratches and the marks…what you might call its history. Wataru, he really loves you."

Wataru nodded earnestly at what she said. To be loved so deeply by someone outside of his family was nothing less than miraculous to him.

"So? For someone so steadfast, he's a pretty flexible guy, isn't he? And then he said that he was too attached to the ring, and he realized he didn't want to put unnecessary pressure on you. He said he overreacted to the rumors about the ring."

As his surprise at Toko's story grew, all Wataru could do was try to take it in. He was happiest that, despite Yuichi's awkward mood, he had still been so positive about the whole thing. While Wataru had been crazy with worry about protecting himself from being disliked or scandalized, Yuichi had first and foremost been thinking about Wataru's feelings. Yuichi saw clearly what was always the most important thing. Wataru was proud of him, and he was proud that he had been chosen by him.

"Wataru, what are you doing over there in that corner? You too, Toko." He must have finally been satisfied, and Yuichi came over to them carrying the ring. Just then Toko hurried off, and he sent a suspicious glance at her back. He seemed to guess that she'd made inappropriate remarks, but he didn't dare say anything for fear that it would boomerang back at him.

Wataru focused on Yuichi. It was useless to try to stifle the smile that welled up, but he did his best to act normal as he watched Yuichi come closer. And then.

"Ahem," Yuichi said curtly with a very serious look on his face. "I haven't given up yet."

"Uh...what?"

"Placing under thirty in the national exams. Is that promise still good?" The rugged honesty with which he said that was inconsistent with the way both corners of his mouth turned up brilliantly. That magnificent, excellent smile was what made all the girls swoon. Gracefully, he took Wataru's left hand and reverently slid his ring onto his ring finger. Even though it was originally Yuichi's, it was as if it had been made to fit Wataru's finger perfectly.

Glad to feel it there after such a long time, now Wataru was ready to answer his question. Just as he heard the sound of the door creak, he saw Miho quietly leave the store. Unconsciously, Wataru made as if to run after her, but Yuichi prevented him by wrapping his arms tightly around him from behind. Holding him, all Yuichi said was, "Don't go."

"B-But... We can't let her go home alone like that..."

"She's fine. Don't go, stay here."

"Kazuki..."

It was unusual for the affable Yuichi to say something so clearly selfish. In fact, this may have been the first time. Nevertheless, confusing Wataru even more, in a voice defiant of his strongest emotions, Yuichi said unexpectedly, "You're the one that she loves. Don't you know that?"

"What?! B-But, she said that she was crazy about you. That's why she gave me such a hard time..."

"She may have liked me first, but you're the one she likes now. I'm sure of it. Her gaze, the strain of her voice, I watched it all from beginning to end. So...don't go."

"You mean..."

"What?"

"Then maybe...that means..."

Frankly, the proud Yuichi didn't usually feel the burn of jealousy. That was why it had been more and more difficult for Wataru, who wasn't used to such rivalry. Now that Toko had retreated into the back, and as the force of his arms became stronger, Yuichi's body temperature suddenly seemed to rise limitlessly. When at last Wataru sensed this, he nodded deeply while wrapped in the arms of his boyfriend.

"Don't worry. Even if the world came to an end, I would stay by your side. I promise."

"Wataru..."

"I told you, that's my only wish."

The bed squeaked lightly as the sheets creased alongside his body as he lay there. Looking up at the unfamiliar high ceiling, Wataru sighed deeply, as if to say, *Forgive me.*

"I still can't believe it. Kazuki, you actually made it into the top thirty."

"I perform well under pressure." Yuichi, also lying on his back next to Wataru, smiled broadly as he replied. Just an hour ago, he had gotten the exam results at his prep school, and had gone straight over to Wataru's house to collect him. Even though Wataru had prepared himself, he hadn't expected it to be touch-and-go after they got to Yuichi's room. His heart felt like the ten seconds before an explosion. However, to his own irritation as he realized this, he had deliberately dived into the blue bed.

But Yuichi was well aware of this. Rather than coming on strong like a wildman, he went with the flow and lay down next to Wataru. You could say that the two of them were in bed together, but they both were still wearing their clothes. Wataru had on what he had been wearing at home, and Yuichi hadn't even changed out of his uniform.

"Kazuki, is anyone home at your house today?"

"No. They went to my grandmother's. My brother and his wife, too."

"I see. How is Takako?

"She had a fight with Puru, she cried to me over the phone about it." He added, "Everyone's fine," as he finally leaned towards Wataru. They looked at each other closely, touching their foreheads together and quietly laughing. The echo spread throughout the room, and for the first time they could tell from their voices that the summer was finally over.

"It seems to me that even though we didn't go anywhere together, plenty of things still happened this summer."

"That's for sure. I had no idea how much of a troublemaker you are, Wataru."

"Kazuki. It sounds like you're still angry with me." Yuichi was smiling at Wataru with a vicious look on his face, and Wataru immediately glowered at him. He was thinking about the grand finale at Toko's store, but it seemed like Yuichi had still not forgiven him for lying about having lost his ring, and for buying a fake in an effort to fool him temporarily. Even two weeks later, he still made prickly sarcastic remarks from time to time. Of course, as far as that situation went, Wataru knew he was totally in the wrong, so he had resigned himself to a certain amount of scolding. But even when Wataru was on his best behavior, Yuichi still made irrelevant comments.

"I'm not your parent, so why should I be the one to scold you?"

"But really, you *are* angry so…"

"I don't have any interest in scolding anyone. Isn't it a hundred times more fun for me to tease you when I feel like it?" Yuichi wasn't kidding; from the bottom of his heart that was really how he felt. In fact, even though Yuichi was popular with both teachers and students, he hadn't taken on any positions. It was the same with student council—he spared no effort to offer support behind the scenes or to prepare speeches, but he never ventured to the front of the stage. Wataru had always found that curious, but this last comment seemed to explain it all. The fact of the matter was that Yuichi didn't like group attention.

"So, now do you understand?" Buried halfway under the blue sheets, Yuichi smiled as he ruffled Wataru's bangs with his finger. "From now on, don't ever lie to me again. No matter what happens, whether it gets broken or lost. You'll always be with me, won't you?"

"Yes, I will."

"Remember that business with the rings. Don't lie to me, tell me the truth."

"I understand. I'll never lie to you again."

As he repeated himself with more force, Yuichi's smile

suddenly fell away. Wataru worried that again he had said something to upset him. Now serious, Yuichi kept his eyes averted, and in an unexpectedly sullen tone he added, "It's not just about the ring."

"Not just about the ring...huh?"

"You heard me. I'm just like anybody else. Whatever happens, I don't want to see you the object of some girl's conquest. I forgot the most important thing. Next time I hear a rumor that has anything to do with you, false or not, I'm going straight after the girl. Imagine the major panic it will create at school. I'll show them who 'that' Yuichi Kazuki is..."

"S-Seriously?"

Seeing Wataru's pale face, Yuichi's smile was restored. He reached out his long fingers gracefully like a musician towards Wataru's ruffled bangs and...pulled down on them. "That means you'd better not fool around on me."

Without notice his fingers slipped from his bangs to his cheek, and Wataru involuntarily closed his eyes at the slight tickle. Despite his good mood, Yuichi said tactlessly, "Next year, our roles will be switched. You'll be the one taking the exams."

"Uh...don't remind me, I don't want to think about it."

"But you forget, next summer will be here before you know it."

"I know. You're right."

That meant that they'd probably have to go through the whole 'will we see each other or not' all over again. Half wearily, half expectantly Wataru tried to imagine the next year with its array of complicated emotions.

"It'll be fine. I'll have my very own private tutor who ranked in the top thirty in the country. Although I think it might be a little much if to try to get into the same university..."

"Twenty-seventh, to be exact," Yuichi retorted, this time holding one of Wataru's cheeks in the palm of his right hand.

Wataru reached out his own right hand and gently covered Yuichi's cheek with his palm. As they calmly held each other's gaze, they could feel as the other's body heat started to rise through their fingers. Outside the second-story window, they heard the incessant sound of the insects announcing the oncoming twilight.

"Are you nervous, Wataru?"

"Yeah, sure…a little."

"It's natural. Actually, I am too."

Both of the corners of Yuichi's mouth turned up delightfully, and as he held Wataru he gave him a short kiss. Then as he kissed him over and over again, the time when their breath intermingled grew longer, and soon it was transformed into a passionate embrace.

As Wataru clung to his body, Yuichi's tongue moved along with his as he stroked his hair and a sigh fell from his lips. Wataru's heartbeat raced faster and faster, and suddenly he felt uneasy and unconsciously tried to pull away from the kiss. But Yuichi was in no particular hurry, and in a whisper he began to call Wataru's name in his ear. Somehow it resonated perfectly with the beating of his heart, and he felt strangely calmed.

He had been relaxing at home when Yuichi had come to get him, so he was casually dressed in a plain outfit of cotton shirt and chinos. But that was much better than Yuichi, who hadn't even taken off his uniform blazer. Now Yuichi quickly tossed his coat on the floor and made quick work of unbuttoning his shirt. Absent-mindedly watching him, Wataru hurriedly started to undress himself when he heard, "Don't do that," and was gently held down from above.

"Okay, Wataru. Just promise me this." Even though he urged him with a serious face, he looked funny in his half-undone shirt. But he spoke slowly to persuade him, rather than in his usual way. "Don't undress yourself."

"Uh, okay."

"And, try not to hold back your voice."

"Uh…huh…"

"Afterwards, don't get dressed right away."

"C'mon…!" Wataru was indignant. Did he think he was stupid? Unexpectedly, this was really how Yuichi felt. The proof was that even though he showed surprise on his face, he calmly and dutifully refastened Wataru's undone buttons so that he could undress him.

It was a strangely loving gesture, and suddenly Wataru embraced Yuichi. The momentum made Yuichi's shirt fall off his shoulders, revealing a muscular body that was thinner than he would have expected. Feeling the suppleness of his skin and his pleasant body heat, Wataru was quite content. His nervousness about touching another person's skin for the first time was dissolved by Yuichi's warmth. He put his palm on his smooth back and sighed contentedly.

"Do you know how lucky you are?"

At the moment he felt the weight of Yuichi, suddenly Miho's voice rang in his ears.

"To have Yuichi Kazuki all to yourself?! You've got him!"

I do know, Wataru answered in his mind. But even though he had him all to himself, he wasn't his yet. That moment was about to happen. The setting sun flooded orange light into the room so that they could even see the movement of each other's eyelashes. It was difficult not to throw caution to the wind and strip down completely.

"Wataru…?" Yuichi spoke softly as he felt the warmth of the palm on his back. Trailing his finger along shoulder blades that stood out beautifully, Wataru sighed without a word. Slowly he took off his shirt, and Yuichi's warmth flowed straight from his skin. Their moist lips met deeply, and they were engulfed in a long, dizzying kiss. Their feelings were conveyed by the force of their embrace, and he granted his wish with a sigh.

He would hold him like this moment, forever.

He would be here with him, forever.

"Wataru, are you okay? Your heart is beating so fast…"

"So is yours. Didn't you notice? Two hearts beat as one."

"Uh, I…"

"I love you, Kazuki. Now and forever." His voice had grown hoarse with passion. Wataru felt as if his cells were changing just by the touch of his bare skin. His whole self dissolved in the warmth, and he was reborn from where he had touched Yuichi. Whatever pleasures lurked, whatever movements were stirred, all of them would be awakened by Yuichi's fingers and tongue. Wataru thrashed on top of the sheets like a fish, moaning into the bed. As his body temperature rose, the places on his body revealed the traces of each kiss, and Yuichi murmured under his breath how beautiful it was. *No one has ever called me beautiful,* Wataru replied as he panted wildly, and Yuichi laughed as his fingertips touched him everywhere.

His skin was tinged with dampness and over and over he lost himself to this pleasure that coursed through him to his fingertips. Suddenly, Yuichi purposely stopped his caresses. Wataru, fully aroused, raised his brows and stared at Yuichi with agitation. His lips parted slightly, and in a faint voice he tried to plead for his touch. His sweaty bangs were stuck to his forehead and his face glistened with a sheen from the tingling sensations.

"Wataru…"

"…Yes?"

"Is it all right…like this?"

Wataru gave the barest nod to Yuichi's question and closed his eyes. But still, when he put his hands on his knees and tried to spread his legs, he resisted unconsciously. Yuichi didn't rush him, and lightly kissing him on his temple, he carefully pushed inside Wataru. Breathing shallowly and then deeply, he bore up against a dull pain that coursed from his hips to his back, and Wataru took in all of Yuichi.

He thought the ardor had subsided, but it flared back up as he moved along with Yuichi. The place of their union ached warmly, and now Wataru tried to concentrate on this feeling. He clung to Yuichi's bare shoulder as he was passionately rocked, while he called out Yuichi's name. Later he became aware of the sound of his own name in his ear. As Yuichi's movements heightened, the mass of heat in his body seemed to seek a release as he rose up. The next moment he reached his limit, and Wataru let out a short cry as all of the heat dissipated.

Yuichi then reached his climax, and he slumped heavily on top of Wataru. With surprising speed, a drowsiness spread all the way to his fingernails, and Wataru was overcome by the reverberations of pain and pleasure.

"Whew."

Unable to move, Wataru stared vacantly up at the ceiling. Yuichi moved his body to the side and he heard him let out a long sigh. Wataru's heart ached with sweetness at the tenderness that echoed in the hoarse sound. Yuichi had kissed him everywhere, and his skin had still not forgotten those caresses. His body was keenly aware of the extraordinary feeling of having been tasted all over.

"…Wataru, was that okay?"

"What…?"

"I may have been a little overzealous. It was the first time, too."

Coming back to himself, Wataru tried to smile instead of telling him not to worry. What had Yuichi just said? Did he say that it was his first time, too?

"Uh…um…"

"Hmm…?"

"Kazuki, you were so amazing… I thought that…" Wataru mumbled with a blank look, and Yuichi blushed just slightly. He shrugged his shoulders as if troubled, and lightly scratched the tip of his nose as he looked around the room. He must have been thinking about what to say first. Without trying to guess what it was, Wataru just looked at his profile in silence.

"I mean…" Yuichi said hoarsely. "Strictly speaking, it's the first time I've ever slept with anyone."

"What about *not* strictly speaking?"

"I've never made love before. I told you, I was nervous, too." His voice returned to normal while he was speaking. But to Wataru's ear, something sounded different to him. It may have just been the timbre of his voice, or the pace of his words. He had never heard a more pleasing sound.

Unaware of the impression he had made, Yuichi slowly sat up in the bed. Wataru did as he had been told and remained undressed. Nestled in the sheets up to his shoulders, he took a good look at Yuichi's body and realized that the room was now in total darkness. The sun was setting earlier and earlier each day. Touched by this, Wataru softly tugged on Yuichi's left arm.

"What is it?"

"If you were speaking *strictly* then…"

"Why are you still stuck on that?"

"Will you tell me sometime?"

For a moment the speechless Yuichi was reflected in Wataru's black eyes as he looked up at him. He smiled silently, and taking Wataru's left hand, he softly kissed his ring. Even the warmth of his lips felt different to Wataru. It could charm him out of any serious argument or stubborn feelings. Seeing him now, there wasn't a single thing—not his hair, his eyes, his face—that was the same as before.

But what about himself? Losing himself in his own thoughts, Yuichi seemed to read his mind as he mumbled under his breath, "It's as if you've been sprinkled with sorrow." Wataru's body flushed with self-consciousness and he sprang upright.

Out of the corner of his eye, he saw their clothes strewn about. It looked a little like an old movie, Wataru thought.

"Hey, Kazuki. Do you think something's different about us?" He wondered whether Yuichi had been thinking the same thing. As he tentatively asked the question, Yuichi nodded his head in agreement.

"I know what you mean. At the very least, I know I'm different."

"How so?"

"My uniform is all crumpled. What happened to the elite student?" The words were melodramatic but the delivery was comedic. Wataru caught his smile, and at that moment the discarded crumpled coat was the most precious thing in the world.

Summer ends and autumn begins.

How many seasons would this love that began in early summer survive?

Wataru found the answer in the intertwined fingers of their embrace. Over time, the rings that adorned their ring fingers were burnished by the excitement, the jealousy, and the passionate kisses, and were theirs alone.

And if the day came when the rings were no more, they would glimmer in Wataru's heart. They would glimmer there forever.

Only The Ring Finger Knows

Vol.2

The Left Hand Dreams of Him

Summer 2006

Afterword

Hello. My name is Satoru Kannagi. Thank you for reading the book in your hands right now. I hope you enjoyed it. I wrote this Afterword because I'm looking forward to your reaction.

First I'd like to talk about the characters in the novel. I am a huge fan of the renowned illustrator, Ms. Odagiri, and I am thrilled that she was able to help us create this revised paperback edition. She is very busy and I am grateful. She drew all of the characters with so much charm, but my favorite, of course, is Yuichi. Not only beautiful, he's such a handsome guy who encapsulates many graces. I hope all you readers like him as much as I do. If they weren't characters I had created, I'm sure I'd be their biggest otaku.

The first episode in this novel is based on real life. But when I tried to write the story, the nature of it changed completely. What really happened was, someone lost a ring they had been given while traveling, and days later, the person who found it and the person who lost it both went to same place to inquire about it. The thing is, the person who had found the ring also happened to have lost their ring. Because of that, both were able to get their rings back. See, it's completely different, isn't it? When I heard this story (it happened to a friend), I thought I'd like to write something about the meaningfulness of rings. With *shonen ai* (a young male love story), how would I work in their paired rings? I thought maybe with the uncertainty of love, they might want something that would serve as evidence. Since most of you readers are female, you probably have lots of memories and associations with rings, and would surely be able to sympathize with many of Yuichi's and Wataru's feelings… Of course, it's not only rings that are important—when it's from someone you love, anything is like a treasure.

One more thing. It's written in the book that the ring tone when Yuichi calls is "Wish Upon a Star." I love this song. You know how Wataru always feels dizzy from Yuichi's love…(smile). There's nothing more painful than not being able to see the one you love. Isn't that what Agnes Chan said? Be with the one you love, or something. Oh well, I'm showing my age, I guess.

That's all for now! As always, I am indebted to my editor, who knew things about the characters' feelings that even I wasn't aware of; it was uncanny…(smile). Thank you for putting up with everything. And to all the readers, I hope you are looking forward to reading the next book. Please be patient.

Until next time, I wish you the best. I hope you all have a wonderful summer.

–*Satoru Kannagi*

WHO AM I?

COLD SLEEP

a novel

by Narise Konohara

Having lost his memory in an accident, Toru Takahisa tries to reclaim his past. Fujishima is the man that takes Toru in, claiming to be his friend. Find out what happens in this exciting new novel.

DMP

DIGITAL MANGA PUBLISHING

yaoi-manga.com
The girls only sanctuary

ISBN# 1-56970-887-8 $8.95

Don't Worry Mama

a novel

Stranded...

Yuichi and his spoiled boss, Imakura, are mistakenly left behind on a deserted island. Can they survive until someone notices they're missing?

One of the most popular "boy's love" stories returns as a novel, and includes a bonus story, "Present."

ISBN# 1-56970-886-X $8.95

DMP
DIGITAL MANGA
PUBLISHING
yaoi-manga.com
The girls only sanctuary